It's Not Complicated!

WHAT I KNOW FOR SURE ABOUT HELPING OUR STUDENTS OF COLOR BECOME SUCCESSFUL READERS

Phyllis C. Hunter

New York • Toronto • London • Auckland • Sydney
Mexico City • New Delhi • Hong Kong • Buenos Aires

Dedication

In Memory of

- My late husband of 34 years, Andrew (1946–2006), who lovingly supported me in everything I did.
- My mother, Maxine Hess (1919–1976), who taught me the value of education and sacrificed to pay for it.
- To my late Daddy, O. B. Hess (1925–2011), who encouraged me to use my education to benefit our community and to become a business owner.

Last and most important, I dedicate this book to my son, Andrew Hunter, M.D., whom I taught to read before he went to kindergarten in the hope that he would carry on the family tradition of the love of reading—even though it may be reading electronic screens as much as books.

Acknowledgments

I acknowledge the visionary Greg Worrell, President of Scholastic Classroom & Community Group, who made the decision to publish my book, and I want to thank Patrick Daley, Vice President and Publisher of Scholastic Classroom & Community Group, for encouraging me to be myself in this book and generate my own unbridled voice. Finally, I give much love to Lois Bridges, my editor, who invited me to her California home, which I call Rosemary Villa, and listened to my thoughts and stories for three full days, and never let me quit. I respect and appreciate the herculean effort of time and attention she has given this project.

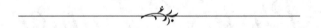

Photo credits: p. 12 (top), Patricia Barrett Dragan; p. 13, Michael McGuffee; p. 30, Townsend Press; p. 32, Constance Myers; p. 40, © Michaeljung/BigStockphoto; p. 42, © santosha/iStockPhoto; p. 55, © Tim Pannell/Corbis; p. 62, © Image Source/Corbis; p. 64, © Laura Dwight/Corbis; p. 67 (bottom), Chris Chow; p. 75, Michael McGuffee; p. 76, © monkeybusinessimages/BigStockphoto; p. 77, Chris Chow; p. 106, © KidStock/Blend Images/Corbis; p. 112, © Patrik Giardino/Corbis; p. 128, © JGI/Jamie Grill/Blend Images/Corbis; all other images © Scholastic Inc.

Cover Designer: Brian LaRossa; Cover Photographer: Todd Spoth
Editor: Lois Bridges; Copy/Production Editor: Danny Miller
Interior Designer: Sarah Morrow

ISBN: 978-0-545-43930-5

Table of Contents

▲ *Texas literacy expert Phyllis C. Hunter speaks to delegates about the importance of education.*

To Phyllis and Andrew Hunter With best wishes

(clockwise from upper left) Drew's Graduation from Georgetown Medical School; Principal Hunter's Men Mentoring Boys Program, Shepherd Elementary; Girls Rock at Math, Shepherd Elementary; Christmas in the White House—while I am a Democrat, I worked closely with President Bush to help improve education; "Reading Is the New Civil Right," a speech I gave at the Republican National Convention, Kansas City, 2000.

Dear Reader,

I'm so glad that fate has placed this book in your hands. We need you to combine the things I know for sure with the things you know for sure to help all students of color become successful readers. If Nelson Mandela can leave prison and become president of the country that imprisoned him, if man can reach the moon, if the Boston Red Sox can break a 90-year losing streak, then surely we can help all kids to become readers.

Our kids need you to read this book and discuss its contents with other teachers, educators, parents, and community members who are positioned to help our kids. Agree or disagree, but don't be complacent. Make a difference for the one kid that is six inches from you. You will find research that convinces you, proven strategies that work, and stories that move you. I feel good—you have come to the right place.

Phyllis C. Hunter

Our destinies are tied to all of our kids doing well.

Our Kids Need Support to Become Successful Readers

*A*s a presenter at education conferences and workshops for many years, I opened every speech quoting one of James Brown's most famous lyrics: *I feel good!* I want to start by saying I feel good about everyone who cares about the reading success of students of color. In this guide, drawing inspiration from Oprah, I share twelve things I know for sure about how to help our students of color become successful readers. I've been involved in education for more than 40 years. I've been an advisor, consultant, and professional developer in the area of reading for many educational stakeholders. As a practitioner, my positions have included teacher, speech and language therapist, and special education instructor—plus, I am a parent and I was an elementary school principal, middle school assistant principal, Reading Manager under former Secretary of Education Rod Paige, and advisor to the President of the United States. I know what works. And you know what? *It's not complicated!*

Everything in my background has prepared me for this work. I couldn't speak to teachers of reading if I hadn't been a reading teacher. I couldn't ask working parents to pull their children into their laps and read aloud to them for a thousand hours if I hadn't read the *Animal ABCs* and *The Chronicles of Narnia* a thousand times to my own son. I couldn't talk to principals about buying books for classrooms if I had not done this for 225 schools in the Houston Independent School District as the Reading Manager. I would not emphatically believe in including phonemic awareness activities in K–2 if I hadn't been a speech and language therapist. And, being a person of color, I have always paid attention to the reading habits of our students of color. What's more, my daddy, one of ten children, was a sharecropper. He moved from Brownsville, Tennessee, to Chicago with the money he earned from growing and selling okra and created a whole new promising life for his wife and children. He had the kind of drive to succeed that we want all children of color to have.

My son, Andrew Hunter, M.D.

Reading is our legacy. Let's not forget what enslaved people endured in order to learn to read, sacrificing sleep—and, for that matter, risking their lives—to attend classes late at night after their masters were in bed. As former Virginia slave John Washington wrote after the Civil War, blacks put reading and writing "near the top of the list of the most sought after fruits of liberty, alongside family reconstitution and land ownership" (Burrell, 2010, p. 170). Education was widely regarded as the one surefire path to equality. W. E. B. DuBois noted that from 1866 to 1870, former slaves contributed nearly $800,000 to open their own schools. University of North Carolina professor Heather Williams writes:

> *It made perfect sense that someone who had climbed into a hole in the woods to attend school would, in freedom, sacrifice time and money to build a schoolhouse. It rang true that people who waited up until ten o'clock at night to sneak off to classes on the plantation would want to establish schools in the open as soon as they possibly could.* (Burrell, p. 171)

Unfortunately, in today's world, reading doesn't always work out for our students of color—for a series of complex reasons, including the challenges of poverty and learned helplessness. However, I know and have taught many successful black students. Indeed, as my Dartmouth- and Georgetown-trained doctor son would remind me, not all students of color are failing. We're talking about *some* students of color, not all. We need to be very careful about the assumptions we make. We can create suicide with assumicide.

Still, statistics suggest that too many of our students of color are not reaching their full potential:

- According to recent data, one in four kids in the U.S. did not graduate from high school. The odds were even worse for African American and Hispanic students, nearly 50 percent of whom did not receive a diploma (Stillwell, 2010).

- The statistics for African American males are particularly alarming. According to every standardized measurement of academic success, African American males consistently appear at the bottom. And too many go straight from school failure to imprisonment (Eckholm, 2006).

- Between 1980 and 2000, the number of prison inmates in the United States grew from 500,000 to more than two million; while African Americans are only about 13 percent of the U.S. population, they comprise 50 percent of the prison population (Eckholm, 2006).

- By the year 2020, if we keep on the same trend we are on now, the number of African American males who are incarcerated will exceed the number that were enslaved in the United States (Fowler, 2007).

While teaching is supposed to be about nurturing *all* students and helping them reach their fullest potential, sadly, our education system does not always serve all communities equally. Due to limited resources such as money, time, as well as know-how and understanding, I have seen many students fall through the cracks or become tracked in a system that leads to the so-called "achievement gap." This gap perpetuates a cycle of injustice in our society that often begins in middle school with suspension practices. Research from Daniel Losen and Russell Skiba (2010) shows that African American children are suspended far more frequently than white children, in general, with especially high racial differences in middle school, causing them to miss valuable class time during a crucial period in their academic and social development.

Furthermore, they "found that 28.3 percent of black males, on average, were suspended at least once during a school year, nearly three times the 10 percent rate for white males" (p. 3). These numbers are unacceptable. They are a reminder that there are still very serious issues of discrimination that need to be addressed, both in the classroom and beyond.

I wish all nine-year-old black males could read the book, *More Than Anything Else* by Marie Bradby. It is the story of how Booker T. Washington learned to read. The book opens with a young boy working in the salt mines. He knows hard work. A stranger with a brown face comes to town. He reads a newspaper to the men in the center of town. This young boy is mesmerized with the wonder of reading and believes, if given the chance, he could do it, too. His mother sneaks him a book. He tries to make sense of the words at night by firelight. Then, the man with the brown face comes to town again, and he explains the sounds the lines make. The boy feels like he's been baptized in the river. The man asks him his name and draws the letters BOOKER in the salt. Said Booker: *I felt like I'd gone to heaven.*

My first job as a speech therapist was at the Moseley School for Socially Maladjusted Boys, in Chicago, on South Lafayette Avenue. The name of the school guarantees that you're not going to get the best teachers; they got me because I was brand new and eager to break into the profession with my first job. Darrell was sent to me because he was a nonreader. His oral language came from the street, and he didn't have the extensive vocabulary he should have had for his age and grade; for example, he didn't seem to know opposites such as *wide* versus *narrow.* Chances are he had never been read to, since oral language, in general, is "impoverished" compared to written language; that is, written language carries far more academically-challenging words than our every day conversation (Cunningham & Stanovich, 1998), Darrell's vocabulary was not as wide and deep as it should have been.

Still, Darrell was a smart kid—indeed, an ingenious one. Once, when the railroad safety gate got stuck, he lifted it up to let cars pass. The grateful drivers handed Darrell dollar bills as a show of their appreciation. It didn't take Darrell long to realize that if he could get the gate to go down and stay down, he'd have a nice gig making pocket money. So he figured out how to throw a brick onto the track in a specific, strategic way that triggered the gate to drop—and he was in business. Darrell happily offered to lift the gate up for drivers in a rush to reach their destination—in exchange for a dollar tip.

Beating the Odds

So I ask you, as I asked myself at the time, how could this smart kid figure out this clever (albeit illegal) "business," but not figure out reading? Again, it was likely a combination of factors; he had grown up in a household forced to grapple with the challenges of poverty, he had not developed the sort of rich vocabulary that's possible only through an immersion in written language, and he was shuttled off to a school with a name that shouts to the world: *Failure!* And if no one believes in you—in your smarts, in your ability to grow and learn and change—it's very challenging to believe in yourself. Having the self-confidence that comes with a

It's Not Complicated! © 2012 by Phyllis C. Hunter, Scholastic

growth mindset, as Dr. Carol Dweck outlines in her seminal work, as opposed to a *fixed mindset* (I only have what I was born with and can't progress beyond it), makes all the difference between those who succeed and those who don't (2006).

Michael Oher, or "Big Mike" as he was known, the outstanding football player showcased in the popular movie, *The Blind Side*, starring Sandra Bullock, makes this point repeatedly in his book, *I Beat the Odds: From Homelessness to the Blind Side and Beyond* (2011). He urges young kids of color who look up to him to outline and pursue their own specific goals.

Having some kind of goal is absolutely essential for kids trapped in poverty and bad family situations, because if we can't hope that things might be better someday, then we basically lose a reason to live. It's a lot easier to fall down, or to stay where you are, than it is to fight gravity by trying to pull yourself up. Having a dream can be the first and most important step in making it out of the system (p. 87).

But Oher also distinguishes between kids who *want* to become something and kids who are *working* to become something: dreaming and setting specific goals for yourself is key—as is never giving up and giving it everything you've got to succeed.

It's Not Complicated

This book is about helping our students of color, who often face uniquely difficult challenges, believe in themselves as creative, competent, successful readers, writers, and learners. And it's about us, the teachers, administrators, parents, and all who care about our students of color and work so hard to help them succeed. Together, we all face tough challenges. And together, as we explore the research, embrace the standards, and work hard to provide the very best support both at home and at school, we can overcome.

Our work is urgent. As Andrés A. Alonso, Baltimore School District's Chief Executive Officer says: "In many school systems, kids can leave and drop out, and it's treated as a nonevent. I want everybody to feel an electric charge when a kid fails to show up" (2010).

And that sums up my aim for this book—by the time you've finished reading it, I want you to feel an electric charge of urgency. We face real challenges, but they are not insurmountable. We just need to be smart and strategic about how we direct our energy. Read my twelve points for helping our students of color succeed as readers; what I know for sure, after more than 40 years on the front lines, will help you generate a powerful and effective plan of action to harness and direct your teaching energy.

The need is urgent and the time to act is now. As Maya Angelou says: *When we know better, we do better.* And that's my aim for you: After reading this guide, you will know better and do better.

Why We Teach:
Learning, Laughter, Love, and
the Power to Transform Lives

by Linda Alston

I guarantee that you will find peace and inspiration in your teaching day as award-winning veteran teacher Linda Alston helps you realize what a difference your teaching makes for your kids and their families. Each chapter includes a memorable story from Linda's classroom, a brief reflection on its significance, and an affirmation that you can use to transform your own teaching and the lives of your students; works for all grades, K–12.

It's never too late to become a lifelong reader.

When Our Kids Are Motivated to Read, It Can Change Their Lives

I hear it all the time: kids these days don't like to read; kids these days are lazy; kids these days spend all their time playing video games. Well, guess what? It's not true. Kids these days are reading and writing as much as ever . . . and in some cases, more than ever. It all depends on a simple question: What do we consider reading? If we're talking *Hamlet* or the *Federalist Papers*, kids may not be reading as much. But if we recognize the time they spend on the Internet and with social media as opportunities for reading and writing, then the number of minutes kids these days spend on both is not declining.

Philip wasn't a good reader. He didn't like to read. But he liked to run, so he begged his mom and his dad to let him run and compete in an upcoming 2K race. His dad said, "You can't run in a 2K race without me." So his dad went out with him and when the gun fired, Phillip took off like a shot and left his father in the dust. After that, his dad let him run by himself. Phillip joined a runner's club. He was the youngest in the club. And he loved it so much that he didn't mind obeying his parents' rule that he get his homework done before he ran. His love of running taught him discipline. And it taught him how to read because he wanted to read about Jesse Owens' life and the lives of other famous runners. He was motivated to read because of his interest in running. That passion came first; his interest in reading, second, but ultimately, they worked together to propel Philip to both personal and academic success.

Jessie Owens

Motivation Makes the Reading World Go Round

No reading program is complete if it doesn't include motivation. It's that simple. Of course I agree that a comprehensive reading program needs to cover the basics: phonemic and phonological awareness, phonics, vocabulary development, comprehension strategies, fluency, and automaticity. But even with all that, a program will be incomplete if it doesn't incorporate motivation. Good teachers already know that. As literacy researcher John Guthrie (2008) reminds us, "Reading engagement and reading achievement interact in a spiral. Higher achievers read more, and the more engaged these students become, the higher they achieve. Likewise, lower achievers read less, and the less-engaged decline in achievement (p. 3). It's the Matthew Effect—the rich get richer and the poor get poorer (Stanovich, 2003).

Students can operate at the top of their game or somewhere in the middle. And *you*, as their teacher, parent, or school administrator *matter hugely* in getting them to operate at the top of their game. There are a hundred ways to tell students that they've done something well, to spotlight their successes, and to encourage them to be aware of their own progress: "You know, this is where you were three weeks ago, and here you are now." Or, "You've added this many words to your vocabulary. Do you know that people need to know thousands and thousands of words to be good readers? Now you're one step closer to that. We're biting off one word at a time." The goal is to get our kids—at all levels of ability—to see that they have to begin somewhere, and to get them to say, "Today, I begin."

The Freedom Writers

High school English teacher Erin Gruwell helped her students start anew and the results became the material for a bestselling book, *The Freedom Writers Diary: How a Teacher and 150 Teens Used Writing to Change Themselves and the World Around Them,* and a Hollywood movie, *Freedom Writers,* starring Hilary Swank as Erin.

Both the book and film tell the moving story of how Erin, teaching in a high-poverty, urban California high school, shoved the textbooks to the side when she realized they weren't working for her mostly Latino and African American students. She worked extra jobs and maxed out her credit cards to buy books she knew would appeal to her students. She also brought in guest speakers and financed outings. She changed the theme of her curriculum to "tolerance," took her students to see "Schindler's List," and had them compare the family feud in "Romeo and Juliet" to a gang war. She introduced them to Anne Frank's *Diary of a Young Girl,* Zlata Filipovic's diary, *A Child's Life in Sarajevo,* and Elie Wiesel's concentration camp horrors in *Night.* Each student kept a journal and shared their deepest fears when they made a "toast for change," celebrating with sparkling apple juice as they declared their intention to begin anew. Maria Reyes, a hard-core gangbanger who started class with a black eye, an ankle monitor, and a probation officer, said: "I don't want to be pregnant at 15, behind bars, or six feet under."

Even though Gruwell's principal tagged her students as "too dumb and too stupid to read a book from cover to cover," all 150 Freedom Writers graduated from high school. Many went on to college. Reyes, who turned her life around, asked Gruwell if she could order *The Diary of Anne Frank* in Spanish. "My momma wants to read about the little girl who changed my life," Reyes said.

> *Treat time like money. Grade level achievers can't waste time.*

Maria Reyes

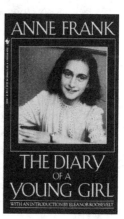

What We Can Do

Practically speaking, the obvious question is "How do we do that?" How can we help our students develop the motivation to become skilled readers who love to read? Over the years, a lot of research has been conducted with real kids to try to answer these questions (Edwards, et al., 2010; Guthrie, 2008; Smith & Wilhelm, 2002). When you put the research together, eight clear suggestions emerge:

1. **Give kids the books they want to read: interesting, age-appropriate, and personally relevant for students.**

   Reading is motivating if you're reading about something that interests you. Michael Smith and Jeff Wilhelm (2002) note that books need to grab challenged readers' interest in the first few paragraphs or kids may give up on the book. Personally, I've never met a kid who didn't want to read about something that was important in his or her life. If you're a skateboarder and you happen to come across a book about skateboarding, you usually want to take a look at it. If you're about to get your driver's license, you want to read the DMV handbook. If the

DON'T-MISS RESOURCES

On the Record

Scholastic brought together the power and passion of Erin Gruwell and the socially conscious work of Dr. Alfred W. Tatum to create "On the Record"—an integrated language arts nonfiction program aligned with the Common Core State Standards that supplements any core ELA curriculum and helps students transform their lives through reading and writing. The uplifting stories in "On the Record" share the achievements of reporters, scientists, writers, athletes, soldiers, and artists, and will encourage students to discuss, read, write and think deeply as they record their own experiences and voices.

Fearless Voices: Engaging a New Generation of African American Adolescent Male Writers

by Alfred W. Tatum

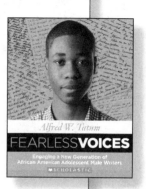

Tatum addresses the power of writing to connect young people with the deeper meaning in their own lives as they put their voices on record, exploring, in particular, writing as a tool to navigate lives in "communities of turmoil" and build positive relationships. Additionally, he examines the power of writing to help students construct meaning as readers as they explore the enabling literary works of their textual lineages.

subject of a text is in your life—that's tremendously motivating (Guthrie, 2008; Tatum, 2008).

Most kids have an enormous range of interests. That means that they need a wide variety of books both at home and at school. The wider the range, the more likely it is that every student can find something that interests him or her individually. As parents and teachers, you know your students and have some idea about their personal interests—so you can provide the connecting piece. You can make the "just-in-time recommendation" to match just the right book to just the right student. The right connection can transform a student of color from someone who *can* read, but doesn't, into a *committed* reader.

2. Let kids choose their own texts.

Students need to know that they have some power over their education. When they aren't given any choices, it certainly doesn't inspire them to be proactive about their participation, because they feel it's already a done deal: "I'm gonna get what I'm gonna get, no matter what I do or what I say." On the other hand, if students can make choices, they feel empowered. When kids were asked what motivates them to read, they were unanimous in their explanation: "When we get to choose our own books!"

Kids like to know what other kids like and think. They also like knowing their opinion is valued. Nickelodeon's Kids' Choice Awards are popular for that reason. There are programs that let kids vote for favorite books, such as Maryland's Black-

Eyed Susan Award (www.tcps.k12.md.us/memo/besall.html). You can use this as a model, even if you're not in Maryland. Just as we discuss movies with others who have seen the same films, we can do the same for books. Make time every day for book discussions.

3. Let students know what to expect with books.

Kids do best when they know what to expect. Take, for example, going to a restaurant. Sure, you might be motivated to go to a restaurant if you were hungry, but wouldn't you be more motivated if you knew what was on the menu? Perhaps seeing that restaurant on the Food Network or knowing that your favorite movie star likes to dine there would further motivate you to go. The more you know about what to expect, the more motivated you tend to be. If you've taken the trouble to identify students' interests and pull together books that address them, let the students know what's coming up. They'll have a sense of control and they'll be eager to read. The truth? Sometimes kids read just because they want to please their teacher. So play into that; say to the student: "I'm glad that you're starting this book . . . thanks for doing this for me . . . it's a good thing. It pleases me." And, of course, as we all know, soon enough the kid will be hooked on the book and will read whether we're watching or not.

> "Group discussion is the catalyst for raising questions that the students might not have formulated on their own. It is these questions and the diversity of ideas and knowledge that capture the students' interest and propel their desire to read and learn."
>
> —*Cathy Block and Michael Pressley, 2002*

4. Encourage students to monitor their own reading progress.

Give kids the tools to track their own progress. Charts or reading logs can help students keep track of the number of books they've read, the new words they've learned, or the amount of time they've spent reading (Allyn, 2010; Atwell, 2007; Fountas & Pinnell, 2006). Those kinds of tools help make the process more concrete for children and give them a way to see their progress with their own eyes. When students are able to point to something and say, "Look at how much I've done," they feel proud of what they've accomplished— and they should. Even more important, that rush of pride can also motivate them to keep trying, so that they accomplish even more.

5. Talk, talk, talk about books—discuss the characters, settings, and plots of stories as well as the content of nonfiction books.

Talking about books can be one of the most powerful motivators of reading. Oprah's Book Club is a perfect example. It

It's Not Complicated! © 2012 by Phyllis C. Hunter, Scholastic

transformed thousands of individual viewers into a community of readers by making reading a social activity. She built "buzz" around a book simply by talking about it. As a result, thousands of her viewers read and even formed their own book groups. Talk about being a great motivator of reading!

Make reading a social activity—you'll be surprised at the deep and complex understandings that will grow from just inviting your students to talk about their books. Discussion gives readers the opportunity to share their unique perspectives and personal experiences. There is much power in a good discussion. People join book clubs all over the world—including online clubs just to discuss a book.

6. Support students with immediate, continuous, specific feedback and encouragement.

If you want students to monitor their own progress, give them plenty of feedback on how they're doing along the way. Sometimes, students need more encouragement to pump them up when they're first starting something than they do later on, once they're into it. It's important to be overtly complimentary when kids begin something new—not in an insincere manner, but by saying plainly, "I'm glad that you're starting this," or "It's going well," or "I'm proud of you for tackling this." Kids respond to the personal note: "I like to see you reading." Making a teacher or parent happy still carries weight.

As students progress further, our feedback needs to become very specific. Just telling them, "You're doing great" all the time might make them feel good, but it's not very helpful. It's much more effective to tie your feedback to a child's specific achievements and make reference to specific things that he or she has accomplished. As an educator, I found that I needed to be very specific about a student's performance and the recommendations I made. The more specific I got, the more effective my feedback, and the more growth I saw in my students. For example, you might say: "When you talked about the chapter you just read, you connected it to something that happened to you; that was really good. It's great to connect what you read to your own life." Or "It was interesting how you connected the character to your own life—it shows me that you have a deep understanding of what the character is doing."

> *Movies help kids develop critical background knowledge. Just because kids have seen the movie, it doesn't mean that they won't or shouldn't read the book.*

7. Use technology to excite students' interest.

Students have a steady diet of technology in their out-of-school activities; it's second nature to the kids

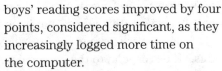

> *Computer use overall involves problem-solving. It involves reading; it involves communication, and these are skills that help children.*
>
> —Sandra Hofferth, 2010

of today. They are texting up a storm and earphones are practically growing out of their ears. I think we can capitalize on that, because it's obviously something that they like. It's the old adage, "It's interesting to me if it's in my world." In the classroom, technology is a motivating agent because it is familiar, forgiving, and exciting. Haven't you seen kids fight over a computer? Technology is fun for them. It doesn't feel like drudgery. It's not the same thing as "Get out your piece of paper, fold it down the middle, and number the lines from 1 to 20."

And now we've got research that links time spent online to a rise in test scores for African American boys. Sandra L. Hofferth, a family science professor, writing in *Child Development*, showed that African American

boys' reading scores improved by four points, considered significant, as they increasingly logged more time on the computer.

Teachers can build technology into their classrooms. They can have students work with interactive reading software. They can use video to introduce students to topics and get them pumped up about a topic before they start reading more about it. Even if a student isn't especially motivated to read, if the technology gets the student going because he or she gets to work on a computer, it motivates them to continue.

8. Set expectations for success.

It can be challenging to focus on positive goals and achievements, especially if we're dealing with a student who's struggling. However, it's certainly worth the effort, because it's far more motivating for students to think about how much better they could be than to think about how awful they are. When we focus on failure, the student thinks, "I'm not good at this, and I'm never going to be good." On the other hand, when we set attainable goals and focus on successes all along the way, then even if the student fails to meet a particular goal on the first try, he or she thinks,

"I wasn't good today, but I know that I can be better because I've been getting better every day. Today I might have had an off day, but a few days from now, I'll probably do well." It's motivating to get things right, and it's also motivating when you get things wrong but someone says "This is the way to get it right. You know that you can perfect this." In my own childhood, I had a seventh-grade teacher who was very effective in motivating me. The reason she was so effective is that I always got *As* before I met her, but then she started to give me *Bs*, and I couldn't understand it. And she said, "Well, you know what? Yes, your work is good, but it's not as good as you could do." After that, I was very motivated to live up to her expectations for me—to prove that I could do the work as well as she thought I could.

What the Research Says About Reading Motivation

Our students of color who are not motivated to read—who are *reading-resistant*—encounter a double whammy:

1. First, if they resist reading it makes it impossible for them to gain the essential knowledge about the world that helps them keep growing and succeeding academically. In order to comprehend a book about severe weather, for example, you need to know something about climate and weather patterns, the role of climate change, and you need to know your way around the related technical or academic vocabulary.

2. Second, without the prior knowledge needed to comprehend new reading material, students are unable to successfully read new text. They are trapped in a downward spiral of failure that just gets worse as they continually lose self-confidence.

Taken from a study conducted by Shana Yudowitch, Lucas Henry, and John Guthrie (2007), Figure 2.1 (page 25) shows that students began the school year with a pretest about science. Within the total group, the avid readers acquired essential knowledge about science from September to December. They learned from reading widely and deeply. Sadly, the reading resisters didn't; indeed, from September to

December, while their peers were reading and learning, the resisters actually declined relative to their classmates. (See Figure 2.2, also on page 25.) In fact, the reading-resistant students almost shut themselves out of future science learning by entering a "long, dormant period of nonreading" (p. 68).

Even worse is the effect of resistance on reading development. As their peers build their reading comprehension and stamina, the resisters slide backwards—losing their self-confidence, too. The end result is a downward spiral, outlined in four devastating steps. When our students of color aren't motivated to read, they:

- lose self-confidence.
- resist reading.
- stop reading.
- lose knowledge about the world and fail to grow as readers and learners.

It's Not Complicated

Don't forget Philip! He was able to meld his passion for running with reading and the two worked stride by stride to build him into both an outstanding runner and a successful reader. As parents, teachers, and administrators who care about our students of color, let's make sure that they have books they love, want to read, and *can* read. Even if kids are reading books below grade level, the research demonstrates (O'Connor, et al., 2002; Allington, 2011) that texts that are properly matched to students' reading ability—that they *can* read—do more to close the achievement gap than presenting our resistant readers with books that are on their actual grade level that they can't read—and don't want to read. But having said this, don't forget that a student is likely to read a "hard book" if he or she is motivated to do so.

Don't let your students become reading resisters! Even three months of reading dormancy can lead to devastating reading loss. With Philip as our inspiration, let's motivate our kids to read, read, *read!*

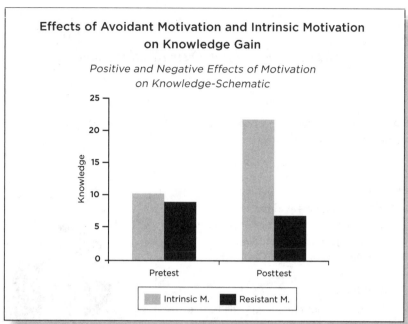

Figure 2.1

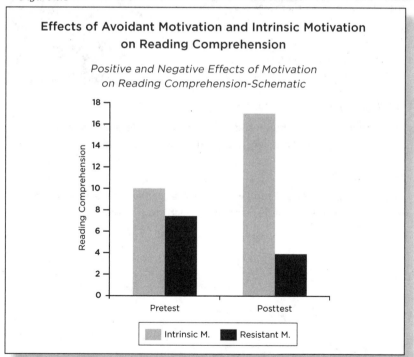

Figure 2.2

From Yudowitch, S., Henry, L., Guthrie, J. (2007). Self-efficacy: Building confident readers. Engaging adolescents in reading. In Guthrie, John T. (Ed.). Engaging adolescents in reading, (pp. 65–86). Thousand Oaks, CA: Corwin Press.

Help Your Kids Find Their Reading Mojo

And how do we define *reading engagement*? Check out these key components linked to practice:

Interest —

Infuse reading assignments with significance and meaning; offer reading materials and experiences that acknowledge who your students are— their passions, values, and interests.

Ownership —

Offer choices that encourage kids to take charge of their own learning and help them develop a sense of themselves as readers.

Confidence —

Confident readers read. Do all you can to help kids find and build their reading mojo.

Collaboration —

Tap into kids' social natures and offer group activities, such as book study groups, paired reading, and group research projects.

Understanding —

Kids want to fully understand what they are reading; make sure you're providing the custom-fit instruction for each student that will make that happen.

Engaging Adolescents in Reading

edited by John T. Guthrie

Reading researcher John Guthrie taps the experiences of talented classroom teachers currently on the frontlines of teaching and the cross-disciplinary research of the "science of motivational development" to give you practical ways to spark your students' passions and interests. The end result? Kids won't want to put their reading books away.

Independent Reading Assessment: Fiction
Grades 3–5

by Jennifer Serravallo

Would you know da Vinci's "Mona Lisa" if you only saw a corner of her dress? You need to see the full picture, right? Our student readers are no different. They need to read the whole text to understand it. And teachers need to see students' whole-book comprehension to decide how they're doing as readers. Jennifer Serravallo's *Independent Reading Assessment* provides teachers with precise data on students' sustained comprehension of entire books.

The Budget Director accused me of buying too many books. I laughed and said, I hope you're right!

WHAT I KNOW FOR SURE **#3**

Our Kids Need Access to More Books

*I*f you are a teacher trying to create a great classroom library, ask the Title I Director, the district Budget Director, the School Board . . . . None of these entities want it known that a teacher asked for literature books for her students and they didn't give them to you. As the former Reading Manager in Houston, the Budget Director accused me of buying too many books. I laughed and said, "Why, I hope you're right!"

Cops 'n Kids Reading Center

Julia Witherspoon is a famous police officer in Racine, Wisconsin, who has won numerous awards and has been on ABC's *Good Morning America*— and on Oprah, twice! As Beth Johnson explains in the book *Sister to Sister: Black Women Speak to Young Black Women* (Townsend Press, 2010), Julia didn't earn her fame chasing down bad guys. Although it was never her goal to be famous, she made a name for herself getting books into the hands of those who need them most—poor children of color who seldom have books in their homes. Susan Neuman's (2001) seminal research reminds us that while "children from middle-income neighborhoods are likely to be deluged with a wide variety of reading

Julia Witherspoon reading aloud

materials," children from poor neighborhoods go without: their families often can't afford books; their local libraries, if they are open at all, have drastically reduced hours of operation; school libraries are in "serious disrepair" (and increasingly are without school librarians), and preschools in poor neighborhoods are largely without any books at all (p. 21).

Julia grew up dirt poor. She was the oldest of twelve children; her parents were just 13 and 17 when she was born. Neither one read well and there wasn't a single book in her household, which was often dark and frigid during the winter months because the family, unable to pay its bills, would lose their electricity. But Julia's Aunt Ruby was a reader. She had a houseful of all sorts of reading material including books and magazines like *True Stories*. And Aunt Ruby encouraged Julia to read. As Julia says, "I learned to read at school. I learned to *love* reading at Aunt Ruby's."

Julia used her love of reading to propel herself through school. She got good grades and, despite becoming a young mother herself, she worked hard, often juggling multiple jobs, and eventually joined the Racine police force. "I knew from the time I was a little girl that reading was power," she says. "My parents were crippled by their inability to read well. You cannot thrive in this society without good reading skills. I arrest people who are unable to read their rights, and I think how hopeless life must look for them."

Julia herself not only enjoys reading, but her love of books has benefited her professionally. She speaks beautifully, with a large vocabulary at her command. At the police station, she is frequently complimented on her clearly written arrest reports. "I write well because I read," she says, "If you read, you learn to write. You absorb the style, you learn good grammar, you learn to speak properly. Using language well becomes second nature."

One day Julia had an epiphany. She wanted to do for the children she served what her Aunt Ruby had done for her. "I wanted to tell them, 'It's okay to read. It's okay to borrow books. You just need to learn to take care of them.' I knew I had to get books into these children's hands. But I didn't know where the books were going to come from." She adds, "But then I went on a burglary call, and God gave them to me" (Johnson, 2003, pp. 58-94).

Responding to a false alarm at a Racine warehouse, Julia discovered boxes and boxes of children's books. The books had slight imperfections and were going to be shredded and recycled. Julia asked for the books, and the warehouse owner agreed to let her have them. One thing led to another and, with Oprah's help and community-wide donations, eventually Julia was able to open the Cops 'n Kids Reading Center (www.cops-n-kids.org).

Today, Witherspoon is retired, and there are 40 centers across the country, connecting kids and books in much the same way Aunt Ruby connected Julia to books. It's all spelled out in the Center's mission statement:

> *It is the mission of the Cops 'n Kids Reading Center to enable and empower all children to strive toward the fundamental successes in life—through recognition for the importance of reading.*

If You're a Teacher, Flood Your Classroom With Books!

" A library is a window open to view other people's culture, but also a mirror that reflects students' own ways of living. "

I am a passionate advocate of classroom libraries. You and your students need books where you can get at them. I want kids to go to the school library, and I want them to visit the community library, but I had a large classroom library when I taught, and I know firsthand how essential it is to have immediate access to a library in your own classroom. The key to equality is *access.* And immediate access to books is a nonnegotiable in my classroom. Having a robust classroom library is a huge advantage for both you and your students. You can hold up a book to make a teaching point; you don't have run out of the room to get it; you have *immediate access.* For example, Devonne noticed that *Little Red Riding Hood* and *Lon Po Po* seem to follow the same storyline. Here's a learning opportunity made possible with a classroom library: "What other books in our library seem to follow the same similar plots? Let's search for examples."

DON'T-MISS RESOURCES

Phyllis C. Hunter Classroom Libraries, Grades K–9

As Phyllis says, "All books are not created equal. Some are better than others. These collections include outstanding titles and award-winners by a diversity of well-loved authors." The Phyllis C. Hunter Classroom Libraries put books in the hands of every student—including books on a variety of levels that cover a wide range of topics, genres, and writing styles that build and improve critical reading skills.

MATCHING BOOKS TO YOUR STUDENTS

A classroom library can be tailored to fit the specific needs of your class. Who are your students? What are their needs and interests? Bring in books that support them. You should have books that reflect all of your students and their wide-ranging interests. Why? Because books are so often our best teaching tools, and we always want the best for our kids. We have a huge responsibility to each and every one of our students. We must never forget that Abdula is only in third grade once!

> *All children must be able to see themselves in their classroom books.*

Here's a story about my own son Drew that makes my point about how essential it is to match books to your students. One Sunday afternoon many years ago, when Drew was about five, we were browsing in one of San Francisco's many wonderful bookstores. I was in the cookbook section, and Drew was in the children's section. Suddenly I (and everyone in the store) heard Drew cry out:

Mama, mama, we have to buy this book! It has a black person in it!

Fortunately, nearly thirty years later, it's not so unusual to find children's books with people of color in them . . . thank goodness!

But Drew's excitement over finding a storybook character who looks like him makes my point that our classroom library is ours to shape and build according to our needs and the needs and interests of our students. Walter Dean Myers tells this poignant story about his own reading life:

As a child who loved to read, I scarcely found stories that reflected who I was. The consequence, since I understood that books represented the values that our teachers wanted us to adopt, was my acceptance that I

DON'T-MISS RESOURCES

Children's Literature Ambassador: Walter Dean Myers

Beloved young adult author Walter Dean Myers is our Ambassador for Young People's Literature. Visit his website for his speaking schedule and public engagements: www.walterdeanmyers.net. Dean's goal for his tenure as Ambassador is to help young people understand that "reading is going to really affect your life" (NYTimes, 2012).

was not as valuable as those children whose lives were reflected in the books." (Myers, 1992)

CLASSROOM ACCESS TO BOOKS: SUPPORT FOR OUR TEACHING

Again, your library gives you and your students immediate access. Your classroom library can showcase what you're teaching right now. Develop a set of mentor texts or *touchstone books* that help you make your teaching points from the pros—the published authors who write the books in our classroom library. For example, if I want to make a point about author's craft—such as repeating words in written language—I might read aloud from Lester Laminack's *Saturdays and Teacakes*, easy to do if his book is in my classroom library. Then we can see how he skillfully repeats the word *pedal* throughout his story to create a sense of time and movement in the picture book (and by examining it, your students might try the technique in their own writing).

> *Kids not only need to read a lot but they also need lots of books they can read right at their fingertips. They also need access to books that entice them, attract them to reading. Schools can foster wider reading by creating school and classroom collections that provide a rich and wide array of appropriate books and magazines and by providing time every day for children to actually sit and read.*
>
> —Richard Allington, 2006

Community and school libraries are fantastic—we love both and encourage our kids to use both by making sure they all have library cards. But these bigger libraries don't compete with our classroom haven for books. All seasoned teachers, however, have great classroom libraries. That's because more than any other resource, classroom libraries level the playing field by providing kids with immediate access to books and the learning they make possible.

In their article "Productive Sustained Reading in a Bilingual Class" (2010), researchers Jo Worthy and Nancy Roser detail the ways in which they flooded a fifth grade classroom in a diverse, high-poverty school with books and spent a year monitoring and documenting the students' involvement with their new expansive classroom library and the opportunities it provided for sustained reading both in school and at home. The results are impressive: Before the *book flood* (a term coined by researcher Warrick Elley), only 27 percent of the students had passed the state achievement test as fourth graders; after the book flood, all but one student passed the test—and he missed by just one point (in Hiebert & Reutzel [Eds.], p. 250).

These researchers all discovered the same truth: Access to books in the classroom has a positive impact on students' achievement. Ross Todd also explored the relationship of school-based libraries to academic achievement (2001) and found that easy access to books at school is especially noteworthy when it serves as support for students' inquiry projects. When kids have easy access to books in a classroom library, they:

- master content material more effectively;
- develop more positive attitudes towards learning;
- respond more actively to the opportunities in the learning environment;
- are more likely to perceive themselves as active, constructive learners.

HOW MANY BOOKS DO WE NEED AND WHERE DO WE FIND THEM?

Kelly Gallagher, a widely regarded high school teacher and author of best-selling books for teachers, including *Readicide*, says that developing a robust classroom library was the best thing he ever did as a teacher. Indeed, following the lead of Warrick Elley's books-in-the-classroom research (2000), Gallagher flooded his classroom with more than 2,000 titles (2009). Donalyn Miller, author of *The Book Whisperer* (2009), did the same; she has so many books in her wrap-around-the-classroom library that she has to

house the overflow in a storeroom across the hall. And, literacy researcher Richard Allington, former president of the International Reading Association, is on record as saying that the exemplary teachers he's surveyed typically feature more than 1500 titles in their classroom libraries.

Scholastic recommends at least 1,000 titles for your classroom library together with your leveled reading books for guided reading. But don't let that overwhelm you. Begin building your library one good book at a time and draw on lots of ways to add to your text collection. Before you know it, you, too, will have the classroom library of your dreams.

Where do you find the books to stock your classroom library? There are lots of places to look. Everywhere you go, there are opportunities to find books from many different sources, for great prices, beginning with—garage sales! As I'm fond of saying: *Don't get in front of me if there's a garage sale, because I'll run you over!*

Nearly everyone knows the great deals you get through Scholastic Book Clubs; you can save your points to turn into great books. Garage and library sales are another helpful book source; indeed, not long ago, I attended a library sale at an Episcopal School in Houston that featured two rooms of children's books. Heaven! But there are also discount stores like TJ Maxx that you may not associate with children's books. My

heart goes pitter patter when I see a red sticker on a book at TJ Maxx—that red sticker means the book is on sale!

When I was principal of Shepherd Elementary School in Hayward, CA, I gave my staff school letterhead so they could write local businesses and enlist their help in funding books for our classroom libraries. My teachers and staff found that a written request on school letterhead is more successful than verbal pleas; people want something to show for what they gave (your request on school stationery serves as official documentation). And, to acknowledge support in a much bigger, public way, consider starting a "Wall of Fame" in your classroom where you list all the contributors to your classroom collection. You can even have fancy bookplates made that say, for example, "This book was donated to our classroom library by Krause Dentistry."

Also, check out online book give-away programs; Target, Starbucks, and others sponsor book give-away programs that will help you fill your classroom shelves with beautiful books.

Finally, don't forget to turn to your students' parents. They are always asking, "What can I do to help?" Parents are your best support because they care the most about their children. Ask them to spearhead a book drive. They can visit local businesses, send out queries into the community, canvass the other parents to tap their own personal and workplace networks, and so forth. Also consider initiating a Birthday Book Program: in honor of their child's birthday, a family can invite other family members and friends to donate a book to your classroom library. It's really the gift that keeps on giving . . . this way, year after year, every child in subsequent classes can pick up the book, note the Birthday Child's name, and enjoy the book donated to the library. And what better way to acknowledge and honor the value of reading? How better to celebrate a birthday than with the joy of a good book? Note: Birthday books work until great until about fifth grade; after that, add the books to a home library.

What Rules Do I Need for Using Our Library?

Classroom libraries, like every other component of your classroom life, will work best and thrive to the extent you take the time needed to introduce it and work with your students to establish rules for its care and maintenance. No detail is too small to share: how to handle the books, check them out, return them to the library on time, care for the books while they are checked out, and so forth. Spend the time needed to review your expectations for nurturing this essential component of your classrooms.

> *The hallmark of a [classroom] library in the 21st century is . . . the difference [it makes] to student learning . . . it contributes in tangible and significant ways to the development of human understanding, meaning-making, and knowledge-construction.*
>
> —*Ross Todd, 2001*

RIBBON-CUTTING CEREMONY

To help drive home the importance of the library, consider opening the library with an "elaborate" ribbon cutting ceremony. If you make a big deal about the library, your students are more likely to regard it as something truly special and worthy of their attention and appreciation. Do take the time needed to help kids understand how to use your library and maintain it throughout the year so it looks just as beautiful on the last day of school as it did on the day of your opening ceremony.

What the Research Says About Access to Books and Reading

We don't have good news about our students of color as readers. The Schott Foundation Report (2011) suggests that

It's Not Complicated! © 2012 by Phyllis C. Hunter, Scholastic

17-year-old African American students read at the level of 13-year-old white kids. And look at the Grade 4 results from the 2009 National Assessment of Educational Progress (NAEP):

Percentages of Black Male and White Male, Non-Latino, Students at Each Achievement Level, Reading, Grade 4, 2009

	Below Basic	At Basic	At Proficient	At Advanced
White	30	34	28	8
Black	58	30	11	1

Not acceptable! We can do better. But we can only do better if our students of color have access to books. All classrooms in our schools need a quality library brimming with books our students love to read—and *can* read. For the complete Schott Foundation Report and more information on *your* state's performance, log on to: www.blackboysreport.org.

This online database is designed to allow policymakers, school officials, community-based organizations, philanthropic partners, and individuals access to achievement measurements and other reports for specific state and major urban centers. In addition to graduation rates, the online report provides, where available, National Assessment of Educational Progress, Special Education, school discipline, and Advanced Placement data. Through this mode of distribution, the Schott Foundation seeks to provide more communities with access to the critical data needed to lead reform efforts to change the educational experiences and trajectory for black males.

It's Not Complicated

Why am I so pushy about reading and giving our kids access to books? Because books—and literature in particular—changes lives. Through literature, students develop:

Curiosity

Kids who read enter the world in ways that wouldn't be possible in any other way. Invite your kids to explore the Louvre with Madeline or sail over the mighty seas with Babar and his bride and watch their intellectual curiosity soar with their reading scores.

Brain Power

Study literature with your kids and help them learn how to read all texts critically—plus, they'll pick up rich, precise language and learn to argue persuasively as well.

An Inner Artist

Some of the finest artists in the country illustrate children's books; help your kids hone their artistic sensibilities with picture books.

A Global Lens on the World

Wide reading across literature is one of the best ways to help your kids learn to appreciate their own cultures as well as the cultures of others.

Better Angels

Our children learn deep lessons about moral behavior—and responding to their better angels—as they watch story characters grapple with right and wrong.

It's Not Complicated! © 2012 by Phyllis C. Hunter, Scholastic

The Book Whisperer: Awakening the Inner Reader in Every Child

by Donalyn Miller

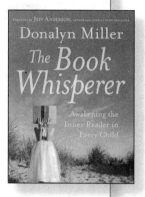

Learn how you can ditch—or at least supplement—the basal and accomplish everything you need to do instructionally—and more—with a classroom brimming with authentic trade books. Your students, like Donalyn's, will clamor for more reading time.

Yes, it's true: Children repeat what they hear, whether you like it or not. So let's make sure that they hear lots of high-quality language.

Around-the-Clock Oral Language and Bedtime Stories Can Prevent the 30-Million Word Gap

*W*hen Drew was in kindergarten, he had a huge vocabulary; I used to test him on the Peabody Picture Vocabulary Test (PPVT), and I could see for myself what an impressive vocabulary he had. I was pleased but I wasn't surprised. After all, I read to him every day, talked with him around the clock about everything we were doing, and answered all his questions as fully and completely as possible. One day I visited his kindergarten classroom and said something to the teacher about *environmental responsibility* and *recycling*, and his teacher exclaimed, "Oh my! So that's where Drew gets all his information about the environment . . . yesterday, he echoed what you just said, and I wondered how he got such sophisticated information and language about being a good *steward of the environment*!" Yes, it's true: children repeat what they hear, whether you like it or not. So let's make sure that they hear lots of high-quality language.

The 30-Million Word Gap

Since the publication of the 1995 Hart-Risely study, we've come to appreciate the benefits of a word-rich home environment in which kids are immersed in morning-to-night oral language, from the moment we sing out our cheery good morning wake-up to the second our little ones curl up in bed for their good night story. Betty Hart and Todd Risley, two researchers from the University of Kansas, studied parent-child interactions and found striking differences among preschoolers from different social groups:

> *On average, professional parents talked to their toddlers more than three times as much as parents of families on welfare did. Not surprisingly, that difference resulted in a big discrepancy in the children's vocabulary size. The average three-year-old from a welfare family demonstrated an active vocabulary of around 500 words, whereas a three-year-old from a professional family demonstrated a vocabulary of over 1,000 words.* (Blachowicz & Fisher, 2007, p. 180)

What does this look like up close and personal? Let me tell you a story.

THE EGGPLANT STORY

One night, after a meeting, I realized I needed to go to the grocery store. Even though I had heard the warning about being in a grocery store late at night, I really needed some salad fixings. I was in the produce section when a mother and her children walked up; the child in the basket looked to be about kindergarten age and, I suspect, the other child was in junior high. The mother looked tired and she was wearing some kind of fast-food service uniform—plus, it was clear she was dealing with a challenging age span with her children. The kindergartner spied the pile of beautiful shiny eggplants and said, "What's that? The mother, clearly irritated, replied, "I don't know. Shut up, don't ask me any questions. I should have left your butt in the car, but it's too hot."

Feeling bad for the child, who should have been at home in bed asleep resting for school the next day, I stood there planted by the bananas. When another mother rolled her cart up she, too, had a kindergartner in the basket that spied the eggplant stack also and asked the question of the night, "What's that?" This mother looked at the vegetable and stated, "It's eggplant, but we don't eat it." I thought to myself: at least this mother named it. The lowest level of

It's Not Complicated! © 2012 by Phyllis C. Hunter, Scholastic

Bloom's Taxonomy is to give an object a label. The kid now had a name for the elongated purple vegetable she had never seen before.

I reached for the bananas when a third mother appeared. This was a businesswoman coming home late from a meeting or event of some kind. This well-heeled Martha Stewart, B. Smith kind of woman also had a young child riding in her grocery cart.

This little girl spied that beautiful pile of eggplant being automatically sprayed to glisten and remain fresh looking, and she asked her mother, "What is that, Mama? Can we buy one?" This Mom replied, "It's an eggplant; one of the few purple vegetables we have. Look at its smooth and shiny skin, its exterior. This is a part of Italian cuisine. The price is $1.99 a pound. I estimate that this weighs about two pounds. At about $4.00 that would be about 1/5 of your budget tonight, 20 percent. You know there is a dish called eggplant parmigiana. *It is like the chicken* parmesan *your aunt makes that you like. Let's buy this eggplant, take it home, slice it open and see how it looks inside. I think it is sort of like a potato with seeds."*

In public school, we teach all three of those students and it is our job and duty to level the playing field through exposure. Remember: it is easy to teach the easy to teach . . . it is the *hard to teach* who are our challenge and responsibility.

WHATEVER IT TAKES: GEOFFREY CANADA'S WORK WITH THE HARLEM POOR

By now, after his appearances in *Waiting for Superman*, on "60 Minutes," and his photograph on the covers of his best-selling books, both those he has written himself and those written about him (*Whatever It Takes: Geoffrey Canada's Quest to Change Harlem and America* by *New York Magazine* editor Paul Tough), most of us know the man—Geoffrey Canada—and his relentless work in the Harlem Children's Zone (HCZ), a 97-block area inside central Harlem. Here Canada, funded by government and corporate sponsors, is leading an all-hands-on-deck anti-poverty campaign to change everything about poor kids' lives—their schools, their neighborhoods, even the child-rearing practices of their parents.

Geoffrey Canada

Drawing from the work of Hart & Risley and other researchers who study child language development, Canada recognized that preparing children for academic and lifelong success begins at the moment of birth (if not before: both he and his wife sang songs and read to their son *in utero*!). He founded "Baby College," an educational endeavor that does as its name suggests: promotes child-sensitive, language-rich parenting skills. The goals of Baby College are simple but ambitious: teach poor parents to parent like their middle-class peers; in other words, to immerse their children in rich language—morning, noon, and night—conversing, describing, answering questions and, in all ways, extending their child's developing language by introducing them to a wide-ranging vocabulary and helping them build a complex network of conceptual understandings. This word network is evident in a child who knows that an *ornament*, for example, can be a hair ribbon as well as a glass Christmas decoration.

For these parents, trips to the grocery store are no longer just quick expeditions to purchase needed food items and beat a hasty retreat; they now represent expansive educational opportunities to "speak fairly incessantly to their one-, two-, and three-year-old children about things like colors and letters and numbers and shapes" (Tough, 2009, p. 201). And Baby College, together with other HCZ educational programs and social services, seems to be creating the results Canada has devoted his life to achieving. Canada knows there are other measures of success that trump achievement tests, but he also knows test score data counts in the public arena, and he's pleased that HCZ's test scores are going up, up, up:

> *When the latest statewide test results came out in May 2009, Canada has stronger evidence than ever that his strategy was working. In the middle school, reading scores finally improved significantly: 58 percent of the eight-grade students were on or above grade level . . . if the middle school scores were laudable, the 2009 elementary-school scores were truly astonishing. In one* [HCZ elementary] *school, 100 percent of the students in third grade scored on or above grade level in math; in reading, 94 percent of them did.* (Tough, 2009, p. 279)

Let's remember: This dialogue and research is not about Susie Q. and Brandon . . . it's about Abdullah and Jose.

Oral Language Around the Clock

It's easy to take oral language for granted. After all, it's ubiquitous—we're like fish in water, so accustomed to swimming in oral language that we hardly notice it. And yet, we're all truly linguistic geniuses making innumerable, complex linguistic decisions every moment of every hour all day long as we navigate our relationships, our work, and our lives sailing primarily on oral language.

It's Not Complicated! © 2012 by Phyllis C. Hunter, Scholastic

WHAT ABOUT AFRICAN AMERICAN LANGUAGE, SPANGLISH, OR OTHER NONSTANDARD DIALECTS?

Let's listen in on Tionna, a speaker of African American Language (AAL), who has written a piece about why her teacher, Ms. Hache, attuned to "standardized English," is the "best"—and why, sometimes, her other teacher, Mrs. Kay, is also the "best." Tionna is reading her writing out loud to Ms. Hache, who sits by Tiona's side to help her with editing:

Ms. H.:   (*reading Tionna's text*) "Mrs. Kay is the best teacher. She is nice"—oh! Nice try [on *nisse, Tionna's spelling*].

Tionna: OH LORD. (*exasperated, since "nice try" to her means "wrong"*)

Ms. H.:   Close. You have the first two letters. Any idea what other letter might make the *s* sound? (*Tionna says "C."*) Good job. (*Ms. H. continues reading*) "She is nice but if you be bad"—let's listen to how that sounds. Do you think that sounds right? "But if you be bad?"

Tionna: (*says nothing*)

Ms. H: Can you say that a different way maybe?

Tionna: (*says nothing*)

Ms. H: "If you . . . " (*hopeful pause*)

Tionna: (*says nothing*)

Ms. H: "If you . . ." (*another hopeful pause*). What about "If you are bad"?

Tionna: What? (*i.e., What about it?*)

Clearly, Tionna and Ms. Hache have hit a communicative disconnect. For Tionna, a speaker of AAL, the phrase "If you be bad" *is* an AAL grammatical pattern and, no doubt, sounds right to Tionna (Dyson & Sitherman, 2009).

As a former principal and Reading Manager, I've been asked about nonstandard English more times than I can remember. Worried parents want to know if their child's nonstandard dialect will hold them back. Grandparents wonder how they can help their grandchildren learn to speak "proper English," and so on. Here's my take: there's a time and place for everything. African American Language, Spanglish, any nonstandard dialect is fine in the home—in the comfort of their own relaxed family and community space, let kids speak their "home language." But at school, in the classroom, it's important for kids to get familiar and comfortable with a more standard "school language." This is what kids do the world over. They talk one way at home, but once at school, pick up the conventions of a "public language" with standard grammatical constructions and vocabulary. Don't get me wrong—African American Language also known as *Ebonics* or the *Black Vernacular* is a full-blown language with sophisticated grammar just like any other "real" language, but it's not a *mainstream dialect*—and not the only language our kids can use to get ahead in the world. We want our kids to be fluid, flexible, nimble language users who can quickly adapt their linguistic style and vocabulary in ways that are appropriate for the audience, the topic at hand, and the pragmatics of the situation.

VALUING MULTILINGUALISM: LET'S GET FLEXIBLE

Just think about your own language usage: you talk to your buddies out on the basketball court one way, but if you should get pulled over by a highway patrol officer for speeding, you're going to sit up straight and use your most polite, if not deferential, so-called Standard English. Linguist John McWhorter (2000) reminds us that language is continually evolving, and every group and region features its own unique dialect; African American Language is no different:

> . . . *words and even basic grammar of all speech varieties are always changing. No one today could have a conversation with the people speaking their language more than a thousand years ago—this is why we study Chaucer primarily in translation into modern English. . . . Language evolves in particular ways in each region where it is spoken and among each of the groups who speak it. As a result, any language viewed close up is a bundle of variations upon its basic theme; that is, dialects.* (p. 187)

As we work with our youngsters with a variety of dialects (by 2012, more children of color will be born than white babies), let's make "communicative flexibility" our instructional goal. Let's help all our students listen for and appreciate diverse voices— through the diverse literature we read aloud to them, and through their own talk and dramatic play. Let's celebrate, always, a *diversity of voices*, remembering that our language

---

Understand Code Switching

Most successful people of color who have been raised in communities of color have what is called *switching ability*. Without thinking, they know what to say and how to say it. If they got into an elevator with white people and someone they knew was wearing a pretty dress, they might say, "What a gorgeous dress!"

But if the elevator was filled with black people, the compliment would sound like this: "That's a *baaaad* dress you have on, Girl!"

It's Not Complicated! © 2012 by Phyllis C. Hunter, Scholastic

also reflects the essence of who we are—our culture, history, values, experiences, and sociopolitical realities.

ORAL LANGUAGE AND EMERGENT LITERACY

The relationship of oral to written language is especially important in emergent literacy. Those children who are sophisticated oral language users with robust vocabularies tend to have an easier time learning to read than those whose oral speech is developmentally delayed. Early childhood educator and researcher Susan Hill (2009) explains:

The majority of African American kids will never have an African American teacher, so I thank you white teachers for taking care of our kids.

> *The everyday spoken language that children hear has fewer rare words compared to the rare words that occur in books read aloud. Hayes and Ahrens (1988) state that the lexical input from conversations are a limited source of learning new words outside of the 5,000 most common terms. To develop lexical knowledge requires extensive reading across a broad range of subjects. Young children's oral language vocabulary, when enhanced through the shared reading of picture books either in English or their primary language, has been shown to strengthen the vocabulary acquisition of English-language learners (Roberts, 2008). The development of children's vocabulary and syntax are related to either hearing books read aloud or from independent reading.* (p. 2)

One of the most important things we can do for our children is to talk, talk, talk to them around the clock about everything we're doing individually and collectively. Remember the eggplant story! And then, besides immersing our kids in rich, descriptive oral language, we want to surround them with books.

As Susan Hill makes clear: the written language kids access through the bedtime story is far more rich and complex than the everyday chit-chat they hear around the dinner table. Kids need both—continuous, targeted, descriptive oral language about what's happening in their immediate world and the refined, magical language of books.

At Home: The Mighty Bedtime Story

For almost every learning experience in which children engage, they are simultaneously exploring multiple aspects of language and literacy. It's the abundantly expansive social, emotional, cognitive offering of the bedtime story that makes it such a potent learning experience for young children. The entire magical experience is truly more than the sum of its parts as children learn to:

- Wrap minds and hearts around the mysteries and beauty of story

- Absorb the music and poetry of language
- Embrace connections between literature and life
- Grasp connections among texts
- Appreciate different genres, such as fable, folktale, poetry, narrative, and rhyme
- Understand the many different reasons for reading
- Develop a passion for books that will support a lifelong love of reading

We know that oral language supports developing literacy—and the more opportunities that young children have to use language, literacy, and socio-dramatic play (acting out stories, retelling stories with puppets, and the like), the more likely they are to become capable, confident readers, writers, and learners. With every read-aloud we share, we have an opportunity to promote their overall growth. Read a book to your students and observe. Do they:

- comprehend meaning (understand and respond to oral language that uses increasingly complex words, phrases, and ideas)?
- follow increasingly complex instructions?
- express self through language (use language to communicate with increasingly complex words and sentences)?
- use language in conversation (engage in increasingly extended conversations following the appropriate social use of language)?

> *When children love a book, make that book come alive for them— visit the book's location, see the movie (if one exists), or act it out. Drew loved the book,* Things That Go *by Richard Scarry. One day, I suggested that on a day trip to San Francisco, we would try to ride at least ten of the vehicles mentioned in the book. We rode in our car, a taxi, ferry, train (BART), bus, trolley, helicopter, fire truck, bike—and cherry picker all in one day. I still remember the look on Drew's face as he was lifted into the bucket of the cherry picker.*

BIG MIKE'S STORY

Of course it's not difficult to understand the easy-to-teach/challenging-to-teach discrepancy when we know some kids arrive at school with a thousand hours of reading experience in their parents' laps while others may never have enjoyed even a single bedtime story. Again, consider the movie *The Blind Side,* based on the true story of Michael Oher, who was born to an alcoholic, crack-addicted mother of twelve. Eventually. Big Mike was adopted by the white, well-to-do Tuohy family. There's a scene when Sandra Bullock, who plays

Leigh Ann Tuohy, takes her three children and Big Mike to a Barnes
& Noble bookstore because she needs to get a design magazine.
When she's ready to leave she finds her kids in the children's section
laughing and reminiscing about the books she used to read to them as
children. Big Mike, who was such a poor reader that his schoolwork
and tests must be read to him, had never heard *Where the Wild
Things Are* or *Ferdinand the Bull.* Later that night, the scene shows
Sandra Bullock reading the stories to him. She was working to level
the playing field for him, and that is what we must do for every kid
who needs it, because every year without access to a rich vocabulary
tends to exacerbate these differences. By the time students enroll in
kindergarten, children from welfare homes tend to be even further
behind. Children from economically advantaged or professional homes
may have heard 30 million more words than their peers from low-income homes.
That's a devastating difference—and that's why we, as educators, must work to turn
things around.

What the Research Says About Oral Language and Interactive Reading

How we read to children is as important as how frequently we read to them. We all
recognize that reading aloud to our children is essential. But reading aloud and chatting
with our children about the book as we are reading it is even better! Reading and
talking about books gives our kids the ultimate language workout.

In *dialogic reading* (Whitehurst, 1992)—or interactive reading—the adult helps
the child become the teller of the story. The adult becomes the listener, the questioner,
and the audience for the child. Think of interactive reading as kids and adults having a
conversation about a book.

Toddlers are primed for language learning. During the last half of the second year,
from 19-24 months, toddlers who have learned about 50 words take off on explosive
vocabulary growth. These "vocabulary-spurt" toddlers learn about nine new words
a day or 63 per week! Interactive reading makes the most of this stage in toddlers'
development when language learning is at its all-time peak.

Interactive reading works! Children who have been read to dialogically are
substantially ahead of children who have been read to traditionally on tests of language
development. With just a few weeks of interactive reading, our kids can jump ahead by
several months.

THREE STEPS OF INTERACTIVE READING

Interactive reading follows an easy, three-step process:

1. Ask "what" questions.

Point to an item in a book and ask, "What's this?" or "What's this called?" Repeat what your child says. Let your child know his or her answer is correct by repeating it back, "Yes, that's a bulldozer."

2. Expand what your child says.

Keep the expansions short and simple. Make sure to build on your child's phrases just a little so that your child is able to imitate what you've said. Add, "Yes, you're right! That's a bulldozer, a red bulldozer." The conversation can continue, "What is that bulldozer doing?" "Yes, it looks like the bulldozer is pushing rocks into a big pile."

3. Ask open-ended questions.

After your child is comfortable answering "what" questions, begin asking open-ended questions. Open-ended questions require more thought to answer than "yes or no" questions and encourage children to use their imaginations. Open-ended questions do not have right or wrong answers. They say to your child: "I want to know what you think."

Remember:

reading aloud
+
talking about the book
=
language learning success!

Other questions you might try:

- "What else do you see?"
- "What if . . . ?"
- "How did that happen?"
- "Tell me about . . . ."
- "I wonder how . . . ?"
- "What do you think?"

If a child doesn't know what to say about a picture, you may need to help by answering the question yourself, "I think that may be . . . " Be sure to praise and encourage, and always follow your child's interests. We need to practice asking open-ended questions, but by following our child's lead, it becomes much easier. Open-ended questions allow children to say whatever they're thinking, which often leads to unique, word-rich conversations.

It's Not Complicated

Above all, have fun! This is just one way to share a book. Our kids also benefit when we read a book all the way through without stopping, which showcases the cohesive story and musical rhythms of language. Then, we can cycle back to the beginning and enjoy a conversation about the book.

DON'T-MISS RESOURCES

African American Read-Aloud

Consider joining the African American Read-Aloud (www.ncte.org/action/aari/packetinfo), which is endorsed by the International Reading Association and the National Council of Teachers of English; more than a million readers of all ethnic groups from the United States, the District of Columbia, the West Indies, African countries, and more participate. Here's how it works:

- Hey, there's room for everyone: Schools, churches, libraries, bookstores, communities are welcome to host a Read-Aloud. In can be as simple as bringing together friends to share a book, or as elaborate as arranging public readings and media presentations that feature professional African American writers.

To be counted as participants, simply:

- select books authored by African Americans;
- hold your event during the month of February; and
- report your results by submitting the 2012 African American Read-In Report Card.

The goal is to make the celebration of African American literacy a traditional part of Black History Month activities.

Whatever It Takes:
Geoffrey Canada's Quest to Change Harlem and America
by Paul Tough

What would it take to change the lives of poor children—not one by one, through heroic interventions and occasional miracles, but in big numbers, and in a way that could be replicated nationwide? That question led Geoffrey Canada to create the Harlem Children's Zone, a ninety-seven-block laboratory in central Harlem where he is testing new and sometimes controversial ideas about poverty in America. His conclusion: if you want poor kids to be able to compete with their middle-class peers, you need to change everything in their lives—their schools, their neighborhoods, even the child-rearing practices of their parents. The book offers a blueprint for comprehensive reform—an integrated set of programs that support the neighborhood's children, from cradle to college, in school and out.

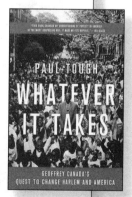

" I know our kids have lots to say. But sometimes, in the words of James Brown, it's lots of talking and saying nothing. "

Academic Vocabulary and Avid Reading Give Our Kids a Brain Boost

When I was principal of Shepherd Elementary school of Hayward, CA, my school did not have a gifted and talented class. This was a poor school. My kids' families paid their rent with the help of Section 8 housing subsidies. There were many times when I had to put the school in lockdown because of some police action in our neighborhood. But I had smart kids. And I wondered why they weren't labeled as gifted and talented. The few I had were bussed to another school. I didn't like that because I wanted these kids at my school so they could be role models for all the children. So I went to our district's gifted and talented program and said, "What makes kids gifted and talented?" And they said, "It's a number of factors but one thing is a strong vocabulary." So I started using every strategy I could find to increase my kids' vocabulary. This vocabulary development was key because many of my kids were English Language Learners. I put labels on everything: cabinets, doors, rugs . . . and I started featuring a word of the day over the PA system. I started to infuse my school with as many opportunities as possible to learn new words and, whenever possible, I taught vocabulary directly. We even partnered with a school in New York—PS 127—so that my kids would have someone with whom to use their new vocabulary. The kids wrote letters back and forth. The next school year, I had seven students qualify for the gifted and talented class. I had just decided to "make me some smart kids!" I knew my kids could do it and they did.

Stop the Vocab Gap

As a former speech therapist, I'm intensely interested in oral language and vocabulary development. And often, both reflect a child's home experience faster than anything else. We can almost always immediately spot the difference between kids who are confident speakers with a wide-ranging vocabulary and kids of few words, who are reticent to share. And too often, a vocabulary gap exists between our students who have and our students who don't. Since poverty and its challenges more typically impact African American families, it's not surprising our students of color are the ones who are disproportionately affected by a vocabulary gap. Yes, I know all kids of color have lots to say, but sometimes, in the words of James Brown, it's lots of talking and saying nothing. You've seen the basketball player interview where every other phrase is *you know.*

> *If our kids hear rich language, they will integrate it and use it.*

And, as this gap widens, it can leave our students of color further and further behind. That's because vocabulary is more expansive than just knowledge of particular words.

Vocabulary and conceptual knowledge go hand in hand. For this reason, helping our students develop a more robust vocabulary is essential. We want to focus specifically on *academic vocabulary*, defined as those words that are key to understanding the content taught in schools.

Avid Reading

Jerry Pinkey, beloved illustrator and the 2010 Medal Caldecott Medal winner, grew up in a small house in Philadelphia, Pennsylvania, one of six children. He recalls his childhood reading life:

> *The knowledge of a word not only implies a definition, but also implies how that word fits into the world.*
> —Stephen Stahl, 2005

There were few books around. However, I do remember, quite vividly, magazines such as Life *and* Look. *I would spend hour after hour looking at the pictures. I also remember stories of one kind or another being told by the adults to each other on stoops, in backyards and barber shops. These experiences set the stage for my interest in words and pictures.*

When we encounter this kind of gap in our students' speech, it's our cue to spring into action and create the word-rich learning environment that can help close the gap. We want every one of our students to understand the importance of a wide-ranging sophisticated vocabulary and become enthusiastic "word hunters" or "word harvesters" as Rasinski and Zutell suggest in their terrific book, *Essential Strategies for Word Study*

(2010): "Word harvesting is an activity in which students select words to learn from materials they read or that a teacher reads to them. In a friendly manner, the teacher or other students help to define the words, then the words are put on display and students are encouraged to use the words in conversation and in their writing" (p. 125).

While much vocabulary is acquired incidentally through indirect exposure to words, especially through wide reading, it can also be bolstered through explicit instruction in specific words and word-learning strategies. Let's consider three components of an effective vocabulary program:

1. A word-conscious learning environment

2. Intentional word-learning strategies

3. Academic vocabulary and direct instruction

Let's consider each in turn.

A WORD-CONSCIOUS LEARNING ENVIRONMENT

In *The Word-Conscious Classroom: Building the Vocabulary Readers and Writers Need* (2008), Judith Scott, Bonnie Skobel, and Jan Wells demonstrate how to guarantee that students are learning rich vocabulary all day, every day—and, in turn, improving their reading and writing. The authors define *word consciousness* as "the metacognitive or metalinguistic knowledge that a learner brings to the task of word learning" (p. 7). They also suggest that a key teaching goal for all educators is helping students develop an ear for language and appreciation for the wonders of new words. Indeed, every conversational exchange, dip into a text, viewing of a DVD, and so forth is an opportunity to raise to a level of conscious awareness the array of new words we encounter daily and can learn if we pay attention. Through the lens of "word consciousness," nearly every event in the classroom is an opportunity to learn new words. These strategies include:

- Using daily read-alouds and think-alouds during shared reading to gather powerful vocabulary from literature and to scaffold it for children

- Organizing literature circles with one student serving as the "word hunter"

- Engaging in whole-class and small-group lively games, such as word bingo and ricochet, which expand children's ability to reflect on, manipulate, combine, and recombine the components of words

- Using mentor texts as models for writing class books

- Appointing all students to be "word catchers" and "word coaches" for each other
- Establishing a classroom community where it is considered normal to ask about word meanings and experiment with language
- Collecting and displaying words in the "Bank of Powerful Language," an evolving word wall that provides students the opportunity to add new words they've learned
- Offering rubrics for word-learning assessment
- Linking reading and writing through step-by-step units on poetry, memoir, stories, and research writing
- Designing a Jeopardy game especially for your class

INTENTIONAL WORD-LEARNING STRATEGIES

Once students are drawn into a community of word lovers, almost without thinking, they'll become independent word learners, and, on their own, begin to notice and appreciate wondrous new words (Ray, 1999) everywhere they go. Still, in the effective word-conscious classroom, your role as teacher is essential. Seize every opportunity to model effective word-learning strategies; use think-alouds to demonstrate your own strategies and offer kids scaffolding tools such as graphic organizers, semantic webs, and mnemonic devices. For example, one student recalled the word *phototropism* by drawing a picture of a photographer and a tropical plant bending toward the sun (Blachowicz & Fisher, 2006).

Use your daily read-aloud to show students how to use the context in which an unknown word is embedded to figure it out. Couple that with instruction on morphology—using words parts such as the Greek roots *tele-* and *-graph* can help problem solve new words while reading. Eventually, with additional support from you, kids will learn how to do this intentionally on their own while engaging in wide reading. Ultimately, it is wide reading coupled with strategic word learning that enables the development of an extensive vocabulary that, in turn, aids sophisticated writing.

Given the ease of Googling definitions or relying on computerized word programs, we might question whether it's still worth our students' time to learn how to use a dictionary. You'll want to determine what makes sense for you and your kids, but again, I believe there is value in learning how to use morphology, prefixes, suffixes, roots, and other elements to break words down. Begin with simple words first to help your kids gain confidence before moving onto bigger, more complex words. As your kids explore dictionaries, they'll also notice all the variations of each particular word. Invite them to become "word specialists" (Akhavan, 2007), taking responsibility for leading the class in discussions about and investigations of particular words, especially those associated with content-rich inquiry products.

ACADEMIC VOCABULARY AND DIRECT INSTRUCTION

The Common Core State Standards are very clear about the critical importance of academic vocabulary:

> *The Common Core State Standards require a focus on academic vocabulary that is prevalent in more complex texts as well as domain-specific words. Academic vocabulary (described in more detail as Tier 2 words in Appendix A of the Common Core State Standards) includes those words that readers will find in all types of complex texts from different disciplines. Materials aligned with the Common Core State Standards should help students acquire knowledge of general academic vocabulary in addition to domain-specific words because these words will help students access a range of complex texts in diverse subject areas.* (CCSS Publisher's Criteria, p. 17)

We have decades of research that demonstrates the extent to which students' vocabulary knowledge relates to their reading comprehension (Anderson, Wilson, & Fielding, 1988; Biemiller, 2005; Hiebert, 2010). And since our kids' success in school and beyond depends in great measure upon their ability to read with comprehension, there is an urgency to providing instruction that equips students with the skills and strategies necessary for lifelong vocabulary development.

Dr. Isabel Beck, professor of education and senior scientist at the University of Pittsburgh, has taken a lead in recent years in vocabulary research. She believes strongly that effective vocabulary instruction should be a high priority in the classroom, because students who are successful in acquiring vocabulary are, generally, better readers. Beck found that words are learned best when learned in the context of reading followed by rich discussion in the classroom. One of her most significant contributions is organizing words into three tiers based on their usefulness and frequency of use:

- **Tier 1** comprises words such as *clock*, *baby*, and *happy* whose meanings students are likely to know.
- **Tier 2** is made up of words such as *fortunate*, *maintain*, and *merchant* that are "likely to appear frequently in a wide variety of texts and in the

Vocabulary by the Numbers

How do kids learn new words? Two forces are at work:

- Direct instruction
- Incidental exposure primarily through reading

But the two approaches are far from equal. While we might succeed in teaching our kids 300 to 400 new words a year—on their own, through reading and immersion in written language—kids learn 3,000 to 5,000 new words through incidental exposure (Nagy & Herman, 1987). But it takes much more than just a single sighting of a word to seal it into memory. How many exposures does it take? 12! (McKeown, Beck, Omanson, & Pople, 1985)

written and oral language of mature language users" (2002, p. 16), but whose meanings students are less likely to know.

- **Tier 3** includes words such as *irksome, pallet,* and *retinue* that appear in text rarely. Although these rare words are often unknown to students, their appearance in texts is limited to one or two occurrences, and because they are often specific to particular content, students can use the context of texts to establish their meaning.

Beck et al. (2002) suggest that for instructional purposes, we should concentrate on Tier 2 words. She explains that most students already know Tier 1 words and that Tier 3 words should be taught at point of contact, or as they occur in reading. Tier 2 words, however, appear often in student texts, so they are the words that can add most to students' language knowledge.

Beck further defines Tier 2 words based on the following three functions; Tier 2 words:

1. reflect mature language use and appear frequently across a variety of contexts;

2. lend themselves to instruction, helping students build in-depth knowledge of them and their connections to other words and concepts;

3. provide precision and specificity in describing a concept for which the students already have a general understanding (Beck, et al., 2002).

What's Needed to Best Support Our English Language Learners?

In the last 15 years, the number of ELLs nationwide has multiplied by a staggering 150 percent. In fact, English language learners are the fastest growing population in our schools. And our ELLs aren't just appearing in our urban classrooms, but in classrooms located in states such as Arkansas, Nebraska, Indiana, and Colorado (Goldenberg, 2011; Freeman & Freeman, 2007).

So no matter where your school is located, you'll want to be prepared as vocabulary development is especially important for ELLs. Poor vocabulary is a serious issue for these students (Calderon, 2005). Diane August and Tim Shanahan (2006) suggest several strategies that appear to be especially valuable for building the vocabularies of ELLs. These strategies include:

TAKING ADVANTAGE OF STUDENTS' FIRST LANGUAGE

If the students' language shares *cognates* (words that have a common origin) with English, teach the meaning of basic words and provide sufficient review and reinforcement. Because English and Spanish share a large number of cognates, this instructional strategy is especially useful for Spanish-speaking ELLs. These students can draw on their cognate knowledge as a means of figuring out unfamiliar words in English; for example:

Nouns		Verbs		Adjectives	
babies	bebes	adopt	adoptar	flexible	flexible
blouse	blusa	discuss	discutir	important	importante
chocolate	chocolate	respond	responder	miniature	miniature

For more information on cognates, visit the Colorín Colorado website: www.colorincolorado.org.

TEACH THE MEANING OF BASIC WORDS

Help ELLs learn the meanings of basic words—words that most English-only students typically know; check the *Dale-Chall List* (Chall and Dale, 1995) or *Fry Instant Sight Word List* (see Rasinski & Zutell, 2010).

REVIEW AND REINFORCE

And don't forget the benefits of review and reinforcement. You can help your ELLs revisit the target words again and again, using read-alouds, teacher-directed activities, audiotapes, activities to extend word use outside of the classroom, and parental involvement.

What the Research Says About Reading and Vocabulary

Building vocabulary is a lifetime endeavor. Help your kids of color understand that you're still actively working on your own vocabulary. Nearly every day brings the opportunity to discover a new word—particularly in the wide reading they are doing across topic areas. Students respond to our passion. Share your passion for word learning with your kids and watch their vocabularies take off!

It's Not Complicated

Let's lift words from the page and make sure that our students become enthusiastic lovers of words. Let's get beyond the "assign, define, and test" approach to rich vocabulary instruction and develop a word-conscious program that helps students relish and understand an ever-increasing range of words. When we become intentional about vocabulary instruction—and do everything we can to encourage a love of language—our students will develop a robust vocabulary that will serve them well throughout their lives.

Five Research-Based Facts About Reading and Vocabulary

1. Vocabulary impacts reading comprehension.

A strong vocabulary is highly correlated with vocabulary instruction (Baumann, 2009). In fact, by some estimates, vocabulary knowledge accounts for 70–80 percent of reading comprehension (Nagy & Scott, 2000). Students who enter fourth grade with significant vocabulary deficits show increasing challenges with reading comprehension, even if they have good word identification skills (Biemiller, 2005).

2. Those who read more have extensive vocabularies.

Avid readers have strong vocabularies; they also spell better, have more grammatical competence, and write better (Cho, Park, & Krashen, 2008; Lee, Krashen, & Gribbons, 1999; Polak & Krashen, 1988).

3. Challenged readers tend to have weak vocabularies.

Reading-resistant learners lose ground on multiple fronts—a limited vocabulary is particularly devastating because challenged readers may lack the content vocabulary needed to understand a more technical, discipline-based book such as a science or history text (Guthrie, 2008).

4. Dual-pronged vocabulary instruction—direct instruction + wide reading—is best.

Instruction that combines direct explanation of words with extensive reading is the most effective (Feldman & Kinsella, 2005).

5. Exposure to oral language improves vocabulary growth.

Just as we can create a *book flood* (Elley, 2000; Gallagher, 2009; Miller, 2009) in our homes and classrooms and immerse our students in wide reading, so we can think of a *word flood*. As we immerse our students in rich oral language and hundreds of intriguing words, we heighten their word consciousness (Scott, Skobel, & Wells, 2008).

Talk Your Way Into a Grander Vocabulary

The New Jersey Orators, a non-profit organization established more than two decades ago, is the voice of New Jersey. Youth from 7 to 18 years of age learn the art of public speaking and effective communication.

Their Mission: The New Jersey Orators founded by a small group of African American executives, understand that communication skills, reading, and academic success are connected; they aim to:

1. build language mastery in seven categories of public speaking

2. enhance self-esteem

3. assist in career selection

4. engage parents in their children's development

To learn more, visit: www.njorators.org. See if there's a debate club in your area!

And while you're at it, don't miss Denzel Washington's terrific film, *The Great Debaters.* Based on a true story, the plot revolves around the efforts of debate coach Melvin B. Tolson (portrayed by Washington). Tolson, who taught at historically black Wiley College, worked relentlessly to place his debate team on equal footing with whites in the American South during the 1930s, when Jim Crow laws were common and lynch mobs were a very real fear for blacks. In the movie, the Wiley team eventually blasts away their competition and hits the jackpot—a debate with Harvard.

Essential Strategies for Word Study: Effective Methods for Improving Decoding, Spelling, and Vocabulary

by Timothy Rasinski and Jerry Zutell

What is *word study* anyway? The authors tell us it's the "direct exploration and analysis of words—through phonics, vocabulary, and spelling instruction," because kids learn to explore words best when we invite them to explore sound, spelling, and meaning simultaneously. Get this book, and your students will learn all about words, inside and out, as they sort and spell, harvest and map, define and design, investigate and analyze, decode and use words—all toward the aim of becoming more effective and efficient readers and writers.

Teach them to read right the first time.

What Happens to Our Kids in Kindergarten Through Third Grade Can Change Their Lives

*W*hen I was a speech and language therapist, I tutored a small group of kids who had language problems. One of the group members was a third grader named Yolanda. She was a beautiful child, big for her age, and what we in the black community would call "fast." It was well known in the community that her mother and her aunt were "ladies of the evening." Her mother had a visible tattoo, and in those days that was indeed something to talk about. Yolanda liked to draw and drew me a picture of a clown once that was so beautifully rendered and artistically mature that I gave it to the principal. I wanted to keep it but I thought it would make our principal go easy on Yolanda, who was in trouble and in the principal's office quite a bit. One afternoon all the other members of her group were absent because of the flu, and Yolanda and I worked on auditory discrimination—which is really phonemic awareness. I would break a word into syllables, and she would put it together. She drew while we played the "speech game" and she told me what it was like not to be able to read in the third grade. She was embarrassed and hated the "baby books." She would not take them home. We worked out a deal that day: I gave her a book cover to "hide" the baby books, so she would bring the books into the speech room and, when the other kids left, we would read them. Today many low-level, high-interest books are available and can fill this need. Let's make them available to the Yolandas of the world— together with a superb instructional program that really fits the needs of all our students.

Let's Teach Them to Read Right the First Time

I've said it again and again: Teach our children to read right the first time. Kids who don't read well by the third grade know it, and they know it's a problem. Turns out that our youngsters' concern about their reading ability—or lack of it—is right on the money. We have solid research now that shows that a kid who can't read on grade level by third grade is four times less likely to graduate by age 19 than a child who does read proficiently by this time. If we fold in poverty, the statistics become even worse: those students are 13 times less likely to graduate on time than their peers of means who are competent readers.

In his study, "Double Jeopardy: How Third-Grade Reading Skills and Poverty Influence High School Graduation," researcher Donald Hernandez notes that third grade is a pivotal point: "We teach reading for the first three grades and then after that children are not so much learning to read but using their reading skills to learn other topics. In that sense, if you haven't succeeded by third grade it's more difficult to remediate than it would have been if you started before then." Drawing from the data of the Bureau of Labor Statistics' National Longitudinal Survey of Youth, Dr. Hernandez examined the reading scores and later graduation rates of 3,975 students born between 1979 and 1989. He found that students who struggled with reading in early elementary school grew up to comprise 88 percent of those who did not receive a diploma. A child who struggles with reading in third grade is the very same student who is likely to drop out of high school without her diploma.

> *A child who struggles with reading in third grade is the very same student who is likely to drop out of high school without her diploma.*

That's potent research confirming what we've always suspected—not being able to read well is a huge problem. But the challenge is ours—how are we going to make sure Yolanda and all her classmates are on grade level?

HOW WILL I KNOW A GOOD EARLY READING PROGRAM WHEN I SEE ONE?

I outline 12 key components you'll want to make sure are in place when you are previewing a classroom for your child, trying to create your own exemplary program as a teacher, or evaluating what you see as an administrator. This is what you should see when you walk into a K–3 classroom, your own or one you're evaluating:

Recommendations for an Effective Early Reading Program

1. *The value and fun of reading well is evident.*

   Books are meant to be embraced, read, and discussed—all day, every day! Promote books! Share your own reading life. Talk about the books you are reading, what drew you to them, and what books you want to read next. At least once a week, when you bring in new books, hold them up and talk them up! Think of yourself as a literary pitch person, espousing the joy of reading, in general, as well as the unique pleasure inherent in the particular books you are promoting. Explain why you love the book and why you think others will as well. Keep it short and lively.

2. *A kindergarten reading knowledge screening test is administered at the beginning of the year. It may include:*

   - dividing spoken words into individual sounds
   - blending individual sounds into spoken words
   - learning names and sounds of letters
   - reading new words (decoding) by blending letter sounds together
   - practicing with words, sentences, and stories that are selected to represent ongoing sound and letter instruction

3. *A 90-minute or more reading block in place every day in first, second, and third grade; 60 minutes or more in kindergarten.*

   Eminent reading researcher Richard Allington recommends at least one and a half hours of real reading every day; struggling readers may need three to five hours of successful daily reading. Children learn to read by reading; there's no substitute for reading volume, which means the number of words read within a specific time period.
   Voluminous reading + targeted instruction = reading success.

4. *Response to Intervention (RTI)—structured instruction and practice for at least 60 minutes each school day, in addition to the 90 minutes a day provided for regular reading instruction.*

   Instruction is framed around three tiers:

- Tier 1: your exemplary core reading program
- Tier 2: your core reading program plus extra, targeted instruction
- Tier 3: extended customized reading instruction; may include work with special resource teacher.

5. *Before- or after-school sessions for all second and third grade students who need more help.*

Basic reading instruction and practice is repeated, as necessary. Summer school instruction is also available for students who are behind at the year's end. The best way to stop the "summer slide" is to make sure your students have access to books over the summer. Send them home with public library cards and a letter for parents stressing the critical importance of summer reading. And/or, sign your students up for a summer book give-away program. Allington & Franzen (2010) have shown that reading just twelve books over the summer is akin to attending summer school.

6. *Reading instruction and practice built around the Six Dimensions of Reading:*

- *Phonemic awareness*: skills and knowledge to understand how phonemes, or speech sounds, are connected to print
- *Systematic phonics*: ability to decode unfamiliar words
- *Background knowledge and vocabulary*: sufficient background information and vocabulary to foster reading comprehension
- *Fluency*: the ability to read fluently
- *Comprehension*: the development of appropriate active strategies to construct meaning from print
- *Motivation*: the development and maintenance of motivation to read

7. *Vocabulary building for first, second, and third grade reading instruction includes daily spelling practice and spelling tests (at least weekly).*

Children learn their vocabulary primarily through avid reading; nonetheless, it's wise to supplement and strengthen through direct instruction in both vocabulary and spelling. The goal is to create a "word conscious classroom" (Scott, et al., 2008) where children notice, celebrate, and learn new words daily.

8. *Reading and writing connection emphasized daily.*

Writing activities are completed regularly and are corrected and returned to the students. By the end of second grade, students resubmit corrected papers. Corrected papers are sent home on a regular basis. Increasingly, all state standards—including the Common Core State Standards—require students to engage in a "close read" of text and write about it. Writing and reading are integrated and mutually beneficial language processes; it makes good sense to connect the two whenever possible.

It's Not Complicated! © 2012 by Phyllis C. Hunter, Scholastic

9. *A daily interactive read-aloud and discussion built on outstanding fiction and nonfiction.*

Invite your students to give their own book talks, and spend the time needed to coach them on the fine art of public speaking. Discuss what makes for a lively talk (and, conversely, what doesn't!). As recommended by the Common Core State Standards (2010), you may want to encourage your students to expand their oral presentation skills and occasionally present and give a complete report on the books they are reading. Again, to guarantee an engaging book talk, help your students master the fine points of public speaking—make eye contact and talk loudly enough for all to hear, including those in the back. And here's my tip for crafting an excellent presentation: you need to *tell them what you're going to tell 'em. Tell 'em. Then tell them what you told 'em.*

10. *Daily read-alouds and silent reading at home and at school.*

Follow my 20/20/20 Rule every day: a 20-minute read-aloud; 20 minutes for in-school independent reading; and 20 minutes of daily reading practice at home:

20 Minutes: The Daily Read-Aloud

Choose books you love to read aloud. Kids need a model of what good reading sounds like and feels like. They need to hear the musical phrasing of your voice as you read aloud to them. As you model reading, your students learn automaticity, fluency, and expression. But, perhaps most important, if you are reading with passion books that you love, your students will develop their own love affair with books. Even though I left my own classroom years ago, students still get in touch with me, and more often than not, they recall the books we loved and read together. There's nothing more magical and essential than the daily read-aloud.

20 Minutes: Independent Reading Time

Now it's the kids' turn; encourage them to find a cozy spot in the room and curl up with their book. They have 20 minutes to lose themselves in a good book. As the old saying goes, it only takes getting lost once to forever know and crave the experience again and again. Kids must experience this for themselves, and once they do, they'll log the hours and hours of reading practice that builds their reading muscles.

20 Minutes: Daily Reading Practice

In his book *The Outliers* (2009), Malcolm Gladwell tells us that in order to get good at anything—cooking, pitching a game of horseshoes, or driving a car—you need to log at least 10,000 hours of practice. This holds true for reading as well. Kids become skillful, proficient readers to the extent that they read—in the school cafeteria, in their afterschool class, or curled up on their beds at home. The goal is to read. If they have chosen a book they love, this is practice they will relish.

If the 20/20/20 rule were implemented in every classroom—together with a rich classroom library—we wouldn't know the meaning of a nonreader because we wouldn't have any. Most of our students who are struggling with reading do not experience classrooms where this rule is reinforced. Under your watch, make sure it happens.

11. *A classroom library of books with a range of difficulty—from books children can read easily to those that are challenging.*

First, know your students. What are their interests? What fuels their passions? Find out and bring in the books that will hook them from page one. The goal, of course, is to ask students to spend time reflecting on their reading preferences and habits; who are they as readers?

- Why do you read?
- What are your favorite kinds of books?
- What do you do well as a reader?
- Where do you have trouble?

- What could you do to become a better reader?
- How do you choose a book to read?
- What book do you plan to read next?

What Is Text Complexity?

According to the Common Core State Standards, text complexity is determined by three factors: quantitative, qualitative, and reader and task.

Quantitative ~

The difficulty of a text has traditionally been measured by its quantitative readability level using formulas that take into account sentence length and word difficulty.

Qualitative ~

You'll make informed decisions about the difficulty of each text considering levels of meaning (literary texts) or purpose (info texts), structure, language conventionality and clarity, and knowledge demands.

Reader & Task ~

Employ your professional judgment to match texts to particular students and tasks. You'll want to consider numerous aspects to achieve the right student-book match.

It's Not Complicated! © 2012 by Phyllis C. Hunter, Scholastic

12. A school library with a wide-ranging collection—open, also, during summer vacations.

Students in print-rich classrooms flourish. In *The Read-Aloud Handbook,* Jim Trelease details the results of a University of Southern California research study that examined the "print index" in the classrooms of three California communities. The researchers found that students in schools with book ratios of only three books to every one pupil (versus the national average of 18:1) had low reading scores and few students went on to college. Trelease explains: "As the research shows, low reading scores have . . . much to do with the print climate. Readers raise readers because they do the raising in an environment that nurtures it" (2006).

> *Trade books are powerful instructional tools. Kids who read get better at everything— including reading.*

Taking a Closer Look at the Daily Interactive Read-Aloud

Instructionally, there's so much you can accomplish through an interactive read-aloud. Perhaps most important of all, it's your opportunity to explain and demonstrate your love of reading. Choose books and authors you love. Share noteworthy details about the authors and, while you want to save time for your students' natural response at the end of each read-aloud session, avoid interrupting the actual read-aloud with too much talk. It should be an opportunity to relish the joys of reading. After you finish each session, you can always circle back and revisit the text for additional instructional opportunities in an interactive book discussion with your students. Use these discussions to:

- demonstrate how to make connections— tie the new ideas found in the text to your students' own prior knowledge and background.

- demonstrate how to draw inferences, elaborate on details, make predictions, and ask questions.

- illuminate the author's use of language and explore the author's style or craft. Discuss how students might incorporate some of the techniques into their own writing. Explore the illustrations, especially if you are reading

> *Our goal is to help children become avid readers who look forward to time alone with a great book in hand. Comprehension strategies combined with a healthy dose of common sense and a . . . [classroom] where children's opinions, passions, and intellects are honored will go a long way toward creating an environment in which children will learn to love to read.*
>
> *—Keene and Zimmerman, 2007*

a picture book, and discuss how the text and graphics work together to help readers create meaning.

- ask questions about specific story elements: protagonist, antagonist, plot, conflict, setting, mood, resolution, motive, theme, point of view, flashback, foreshadowing, and so forth.

- examine the text for its use of grammar, punctuation, and figures of speech.

Note to Principals: When you visit classrooms, bring a book to read. Principal Bob Wortman, who works primarily with Latino and Native American kids in Tucson, Arizona, never enters a classroom without a copy of his newest favorite picture book tucked under his arm. What a glorious way to introduce new books and build a positive relationship with the children.

The Close Read: Comprehension and the Common Core

These days, everyone is talking about "the close read"—and no wonder because, under the Common Core, close reading has become more important than ever. Indeed, what seems to distinguish students who succeed from those who don't is the ability to engage independently in close analysis of demanding text.

To this end—to help our kids build capacity to read increasingly complex text—students must engage in a close read of complex literary and informational text every day and aim to accomplish the dual goals as outlined by CCSS (2010) and explained by literacy researcher Dr. Elfrieda Hiebert (2011):

- undertake the close, attentive reading that lies at the heart of understanding and enjoying complex works of literature

- perform the critical reading necessary to analyze the staggering amount of information available in print and digitally

Rereading and writing about the text are two indispensable strategies for accessing the information and knowledge each text holds. Reading well means gaining the maximum insight or knowledge possible from each source. Rereading and writing in response to guiding questions meant to help students unlock the meaning are essential.

Reading Logs

One sure way to boost your students' belief in themselves as readers is to ask them to keep a Reading Log of everything they read over the course of a week—not just books but everything: Web pages, commercial packaging, newspapers, magazines, text messages, and so on. We want kids to understand that their reading world is vast and varied. While we want to always promote the glory of books and extended text, we also want the kids to track their reading across a range of genres. In this way, they'll recognize that reading is not a pleasure removed from the essential nature of their own lives, but it is vital and fundamental to everything they do.

Steven Layne offers a nice system for log-keeping; consider adapting it to your own classroom (you might choose different "buckets" for the kids to fill). Steve uses the rating box for his own one-to-five star system; five stars is top choice. Keeping track of genres encourages broad and deep reading and also begins to help kids discover themselves as readers with unique preferences and challenges. While science fiction may rock Arnold's world, Sabrina can't abide anything that's not nonfiction.

Reading Journals

A reading journal helps students interact on a personal level with books and authors and is often an effective way of expanding comprehension. As Karen Bromley explains (1993), "Journals provide students with records of their own thoughts, ideas, and observations, and so invite them to reread, revisit, and perhaps revise past thoughts" (p. x). In its physical form, a reading journal can be a notebook, sketchbook, or simply pages within a file folder. Before you introduce reading journals into your classroom, model their use and let students know that you, too, will be keeping one. Besides the conventional response journal, consider these variations:

- **Double-Entry Journal.** This type of journal invites readers to have a dialogue with themselves and may work particularly well with nonfiction text. In the left column, the reader writes reports of information, summaries, quotations, or objective accounts. Directly opposite, in the right column, the reader records associated thoughts—feelings, personal observations, and interpretations.

- **Partner Across the Pages.** This journal invites teacher-student dialogue. Using a two-column format, the student writes comments on a book in the first column and then places the journal in a designated spot where the teacher will find it. Within a set amount of time, the teacher writes

Name_____ Grade_____

Reading Log Selections

Qtr.	Title	Author	Genre	Rating

It's Not Complicated! © 2012 by Phyllis C. Hunter, Scholastic

a response to the student's entry in the second column and return the journal. This is an excellent way to provide individual attention to readers and to help keep them focused on their book.

What the Research Says About the Importance of an Excellent K–3 Reading Program

Let's dig deeper into Dr. Hernandez' research findings; recall, he found that kids who struggle with reading in third grade continue to struggle:

- Low reading skills is a stronger predictor of eventual high school dropout than spending at least a year in poverty, which affected 70 percent of the students who didn't graduate.

- 89 percent of students in poverty who did read on level by third grade graduated on time, statistically no different from the students who never experienced poverty but did struggle with reading early on.

- More than one in four poor, struggling readers did not graduate, compared with only 2 percent of good readers from wealthier backgrounds.

- Gaps in graduation rates among white, black, and Hispanic students closed once poverty and reading proficiency were taken into account.

> *If they are proficient in reading, [white and African American kids] basically have the same rate of graduation — above 90 percent. If [African American kids] did not reach proficiency, that's when you see these big gaps emerge.*
>
> —*Donald Hernandez, 2011*

It's Not Complicated

Linda Alston is an amazing, award-winning kindergarten teacher who works with inner-city kids in Denver, CO. Listen to what she has to say about encouraging our youngest students:

Believe in the child! *If you believe the child can read, let him or her read for Pete's sake! Do not withhold learning for fear that it is too much, will damage the brain, or is too sophisticated. So what if the children are poor, of color, white, wealthy and sheltered, or "ghetto fabulous!" Make no excuse! Make learning fun . . . if you believe in children, that they have something to offer to you, to each other, and to the world, you will be absolutely floored by the insights young children will express . . . . Choose one of your favorite poems or passages. Sit down with the child. Read it to him or her. Teach that child to read it. Open up discussion and watch what will happen. I double dare you! You will be calling people all over the country quoting what the child said. That's a promise.* (2008, p. 132)

DON'T-MISS RESOURCES

Teaching Phonics: K–3

by Wiley Blevins

How do young children learn to crack open text and make meaning of the black squiggles before them? Phonics experts Wiley Blevins tells us that kids need multiple tools that enable them to:

- Map sounds onto spellings

- Acquire *automaticity*—the ability to recognize a large number of words quickly and accurately

- Read fluently with comprehension and pleasure

The Swiss Army knife of beginning reading instruction that accomplishes all this and more is phonics instruction. Research, both past and present, demonstrates that beginning readers succeed to the extent that their teachers spotlight the relationship between letter, sound, and word recognition, and between fluency and reading comprehension, always keeping in mind, of course, that the ultimate goal is comprehension.

Every time kids read they need to ask themselves, Does this make sense? If not, they better figure out why.

Our Kids Are Not Reading if They Aren't Comprehending

We would do well to heed the wise words of Dr. Pedro Antonio Noguera, who writes in *Motion Magazine:* ". . . it is possible to educate *all* children, including black males, at high levels. This idea is not an articulation of faith, but rather a conclusion drawn from a vast body of research on human development and from research on the learning styles of Black children. Therefore, it is possible for schools to take actions that can reverse the patterns of low achievement among African American males. The fact that some schools and programs manage to do so already is further evidence that there is a possibility of altering these trends" (May 13, 2002).

That's what I say: If some schools can do it, why not all schools?

LaKeisha's Rich Reading Life: What We Want for All Our Kids

LaKeisha, a young African American woman who was raised by a single mom and attended a diverse school in the South, explains that reading has always been her "hobby." She said that she read "innumerable" books before she entered first grade and her mom, too, is a "big reader." You won't be surprised to hear that her verbal SAT score is 650 (the African American mean score is 434; for all groups it's 505). This is how LaKeisha describes her reading life:

> *Reading was always held in high regard in my family. I grew up watching my mom read. I can recall going to book exchange events and stores where we bought and traded books as our form of weekend recreation. I have never had problems reading and I began reading for fun at a very early age. Along with the support at home, I attended schools that stressed the importance of reading. I was blessed to be in classes with teachers who made us functional library users. I cannot pinpoint the precise reason for my love of reading. I can only express how much I have always enjoyed it.*
>
> *I believe being introduced to various genres of reading played a key role in my verbal test scores. Reading advanced literature at an early age introduced me to a broad range of vocabulary, which increased my verbal scores. And reading advanced-level mysteries enhanced my critical thinking abilities.* (LaKeisha; quoted in Jairrels, 2009, pp. 94–95)

It's a well-established research finding that students' reading ability is dramatically influenced by the amount of background information they are able to bring to their every reading encounter (Duke & Carlisle, 2011; Hiebert & Reutzel, 2010; Allington, 2010). By reading widely, students are exposed to diverse topics and information, which they can then use to assure their successful entry into future reading and learning.

It's obvious: the more children read, the more they build their background knowledge, which in turn strengthens their ability to comprehend. It's so simple and yet has such profound ramifications. What's more, effective teachers of reading know that comprehension is enhanced by reflection and social interaction. Consequently, they provide their students with multiple opportunities to respond to their reading and interact with their peers through a variety of activities such as book clubs and online discussions. When students talk about the books they are reading, it promotes their ability to think critically and develop a deeper understanding of what they have read. As I'm fond of saying: *There's power in discussion.*

Why Comprehension Is Everything

Are children reading if they don't understand and comprehend what they read? Absolutely not! There is no reading without comprehension. For education reformer and promoter Geoffrey Canada, reading and books played a pivotal role in his academic success and ultimate professional accomplishment. In *Fist, Stick, Gun, Knife* (1995), Canada notes that outside of school, voluntary reading contributed substantially to his school success: "I loved reading, and my mother, who read voraciously, too, allowed me to have her novels after she finished them. My strong reading background allowed me to have an easier time of it in most of my classes" (p. 70).

Fortunately for her students, sixth grade teacher and bestselling author Donalyn Miller promotes free, voluntary reading *inside* her classroom. By year's end, her students read for 30 minutes of her 90-minute language arts/social study block. And all that reading pays off: "We teachers have more than enough anecdotal evidence that the students who read the most are the best spellers, writers, and thinkers. No exercise gives more instructional bang for the buck than reading" (p. 55).

And as reported in *Revisiting Silent Reading: New Directions*

> *Practice. Discuss. Enjoy. Practice makes perfect; discussion increases comprehension; and enjoyment provides motivation.*

DON'T-MISS RESOURCES

Black Books Galore!

Do you love *The Watsons Go to Birmingham* like I do? If so, you might also like one of my favorite websites: (www.blackbooksgalore.com/) where you'll find this book and many more, specially selected for children of color by authors Donna Rand and Toni Trent Parker. These two have selected a stellar assortment of books for boys from birth through eighth grade for inclusion in their fabulous resource for boys (as well as hundreds more in the version for girls: *Black Books Galore! Guide to Great African American Children's Books About Girls.*) Here's how their website describes them:

Parents, teachers, librarians, and kids themselves will find this an invaluable resource, as well as a thoroughly enjoyable reading experience. The authors include brief, lively descriptions of over 350 books, such as Charlie Parker Played Be Bop *and* The Watsons Go to Birmingham, *often including text excerpts and pictures of book covers to impart the flavor of the books. They include several special features, such as "The Creator's Reflections"—spotlights on talented authors and illustrators, from Angela Johnson to Tom Feelings to Mildred Pitts Walter—as well as quotations from well-known African American personages and from young readers and their parents. The selections are arranged alphabetically by title and numbered sequentially for easy cross-referencing.* —Emilie Coulter *for Teachers and Researchers* by Elfrieda Hiebert and D. Ray Reutzel (2010), the evidence is compelling that the Opportunity to Read (OTR) as coined by Guthrie, Schafter, and Huang (2001) is associated with literacy performance. Provide your students with abundant OTR and watch them soar as readers and learners. Truly, books and avid reading are a child's best ticket to lifelong success (Murray, 2010).

SHOULD I TEACH COMPREHENSION?

Yes! Our goal is to help our students become "mentally active" while reading and to reach a point where they can, on their own, initiate the strategies of an "active comprehender." Cathy Collins and Michael Pressley (2007) outline a Comprehension Lesson Plan for us that is research-based and lists the sorts of questions we want our students to automatically ask while reading—depending on what they are reading and for what purpose. In this way, students are able to interact with every text they encounter and maintain an internal dialogue, monitoring their own understanding as they work their way through the text. Note, not all these questions are appropriate for every text (or for every reader); for example, we don't read a poem in the same way or for the same purpose that we read the directions for programming our smart phones. This list of questions is meant to guide each student's inner reader—the one who maintains an ongoing dialogue with the authors your students encounter on their reading journeys.

The Research-Based Comprehension Lesson Plan

Understanding the words —

- Can I fluently read the words in the sentence without pausing?
- Can I use my background knowledge to make sense of the words?
- Does word meaning make sense?

Interpreting sentences and paragraphs —

- Does it make sense?
- Can I recall what I just read?
- Can I determine what the author thinks is most important in each paragraph by selecting, deleting, condensing, and integrating the key information in every paragraph?

Understanding text well —

- Can I see the characters, the setting, the actions?
- Can I use my sensory images to make a movie in my mind?

It's Not Complicated! © 2012 by Phyllis C. Hunter, Scholastic

- Can I use story grammar and text features to follow an author's train of thought?
- Have I looked for the author's writing style so I can follow the compare/contrast, descriptive, problem/solution, cause/effect, or sequential patterns through which information is being presented?
- Can I interpret, predict, and update my knowledge by scanning the titles, headings, and pictures and relating the information gained to prior knowledge?
- Can I summarize the text, making sure my summary includes information gained from the story and eliminates duplication, restates in fewer words, and uses summary words? If I can't, did I interpret this as a sign to reread?
- Have I reread for clarification?
- Have I used fix-up comprehension strategies?
- Are there still questions or concepts that were explored in the text that I missed?
- Can I use the "Why" and "How" questions, and ask questions about why things are the way they are in the fiction or nonfiction story or informational text?
- Can I draw inferences or create images by filling in details missing from the text or by elaborating on what I read?

Sharing and using the knowledge gained —

- How is my knowledge different now?
- Do I need to acquire more knowledge in this area? Have I come up with a plan to do so?
- Have I connected the ideas in this text to my personal reference of knowledge from other texts and general world knowledge, making certain that these connections do not divert my attention away from the actual text?
- Have I used cultural knowledge to comprehend and use what I read? (pp. 227–228)

What the Research Says About Reading Comprehension

Here's what the research tells us about reading comprehension: Avid reading builds successful comprehension, which, in turn, helps assure lifelong learning and success.

RESEARCH-BASED FACTS ABOUT READING COMPREHENSION

- Students who read actively and frequently improve their comprehension of text as a consequence (Duke & Carlisle, 2011; Allington, 2009).
- The amount of reading is a strong predictor of reading comprehension, outweighing intelligence, economic background, and gender (Reutzel & Gikkubgsworth, 1991).
- An abundance of interesting books in the classroom—plus the time and

encouragement to read them—promotes the use of comprehension strategies (Guthrie, et al., 2008).

- Students who are exposed to real texts—books and stories rather than short passages in basal readers—and who respond to what they read perform better on standardized tests of reading achievement (Wenglinsky, 2003).

- Extensive reading of developmentally appropriate material of many kinds, both in and out of school, results in substantial growth in vocabulary and comprehension abilities, and in the information base that students acquire (Squires, 2004).

- Reading a lot serves to develop vocabulary, background knowledge, familiarity with complex syntactic structures, and word recognition (Duke & Carlisle, 2011; Cunningham & Stanovich, 1998).

Do what works! Don't ride a dead horse.

How Much Time Do You Spend Reading Every Day?

How we ask kids to explain their reading habits greatly influences the kinds of responses we get because, often, kids don't define the time they spend consuming comics or checking out Facebook as reading—but it is.

Look at this chart showing number of minutes per day spent reading in various years from 1946 to 2010. Just considering book reading, there is little difference between the 1946 estimate and the most current 2010 estimate. The only real drop is the decline in newspapers and magazines (Krashen, 2011).

Average Number of Minutes Per Day of Reading

STUDY	AGE	BOOKS	MAGAZINES & NEWSPAPERS	WEBSITES	TOTAL READING
Link & Hopf, 1946	15-19	22	42		54
Roberts, 1999	14-18	14	23	9	46
Roberts, 2005	15-18	24	20	19	63
Rideout, 2010	15-18	21	13	16	50

It's Not Complicated

Sherman Alexie, author of numerous award-winning books for adults and kids, once wrote:

If one reads enough books, one has a fighting chance. Or better, one's chances of survival increase with each book one reads.

This isn't a game. Our kids are losing their lives to violence and prison out there. Knowing how to read may be their best chance at surviving—and, ultimately, thriving. Don't waste time. Have high and clear expectations and make sure your kids understand them. Talk about the books you are reading and why. Read in front of them and model a think-aloud: let your kids see inside your "brain" as you puzzle over new words and build meaning from the print. Give your kids a reading log and get them to record all the books that they read every year—25 books a year is minimum.

DON'T-MISS RESOURCES

Revisiting Silent Reading: New Directions for Teachers and Researchers

by Elfrieda Hiebert and D. Ray Reutzel

Silent reading makes a comeback! *Revisiting Silent Reading* brings together leading scholars in reading education who agree on one thing: When independent silent reading practice time is accompanied by active teacher instruction, guidance, interaction, and monitoring, student reading development and engagement flourish.

> "If more than 20 percent of our kids are referred to special education, there's nothing special about it."

RTI (Response to Intervention) Breaks the Cycle of Failure for Our Kids

Teacher Elizabeth Saavedra recalls her student Vincent's response when she handed him a word list and asked him to read it. With crinkled brow, Vincent studied the list intently and silently mouthed some of the words. When Elizabeth asked him if he could read the words, he replied very confidently, "Oh yes, I can read these words. I know how to read." Elizabeth asked him if he could read the words out loud to her. And again, Vincent replied with great confidence: "Oh yes, I can read these words. I know how to read" . . . still, he wasn't reading, so Elizabeth asked him gently if there was a problem with the list. Vincent explained: "Yeah, there is. You see, I know how to read, but I can't say what these words are because I haven't learned typing yet!"

I cheer Vincent's confidence and it's entirely possible that if he were to encounter the words in an extended story he *could* read the words. Still, in every class I taught, I always knew I'd encounter kids, who, for whatever reason, simply didn't seem to *get* reading. The reasons some kids fail to thrive as readers are many and complex. While some are able to read, for any number of reasons, they choose not to; they have the ability but lack the passion. While they might respond to external motivation such as contests for reading the most books or promised rewards for completing reading assignments, they aren't kids who relish reading and who know deep down the intrinsic joys of getting lost in a book. Then, too, we have kids who are low achievers and struggle with reading. For some reason, they haven't engaged in reading in a way that helps them understand what reading is and why anyone should want to read. And the tough thing about reading is that if you don't read, you don't grow as a reader, and you fall further and further behind. Finally, we encounter kids who may have real disabilities that block them from successful reading. While it still may be possible to reach these kids in your own classroom, there's no doubt it's a challenge, and you may need to call on your school psychologist and special resource teacher for help.

Still, we have great reason to hope that we can help all our challenged readers. We know so much more about how to overcome their resistance. And this new information enables us to achieve success with our strugglers right inside our own classrooms. It's a systemic approach that's more likely to help our struggling readers cross over to successful reading. It's called Response to Intervention (RTI), and it originated in 2002 with the Individuals with Disabilities Education Act (IDEA).

Kids of Color May Need RTI, Not Special Education

While the premise behind RTI is simple, its results are revolutionary: Students who struggle with reading no longer face a battery of diagnostic tests administered by a school psychologist which, in years past, often led to a special education placement. Now, thanks to the RTI breakthrough, you, as a classroom teacher, can use a series of systematic assessments to determine the needs and challenges of your struggling readers. With that data in hand, you are able to create a thoughtful program of support for your students who need it—right inside the comfort of your own classroom and using your own core reading program. In other words, you no longer need to refer your struggling readers to your school psychologist and work to get them placed in special education, a process that can take months and can leave kids feeling depressed and isolated.

In developing No Child Left Behind, we knew that kids who didn't get it the first time around needed extra help. As I worked to shape the No Child Left Behind legislation with President Bush, we developed Levels 1, 2, and 3, which correspond to RTI's three tiers. Those of us who work with kids of color know that too frequently they are referred to special education before they've received all warranted and thoughtful levels of classroom intervention. Consider these statistics:

- African American students account for only 14.8 percent of the general population of 6-to-21-year-old students, but they make up 20 percent of the special education population across all disabilities (Losen & Orfield, 2002).

- African American kids are 2.41 times more likely than white students to be identified as having mental retardation, 1.13 times more likely to be labeled as learning disabled, and 1.68 times as likely to be found to have an emotional or behavioral disorder (Klingner, et al., 2005).

Programs don't teach, teachers do!

RTI is very important to kids of color because it means they get the "just-in-time" help that breaks the cycle of failure. It means that they will receive as much as two years' worth of instruction in one so that they have an honest shot at catching up and aren't always behind. Never forget: *Programs don't teach, teachers do!* And, of course, kids need books they love. Getting the right books into kids' hands is the key to intervention strategies that work as well as the ultimate goal—engaged readers.

Three RTI Instructional Tiers

Again, with RTI, you provide the support and guidance your struggling readers need in the comfort of your own classroom, inside the boundaries of your own core reading program framed around three tiers of instruction.

TIER I

Your Tier 1 intervention is essentially your core reading program intensified—so you might engage your strugglers in more one-on-one and small-group instruction informed by the best available information on how to teach reading. CIERA (Center for Improvement of Early Reading Achievement) investigated the practices of accomplished classroom teachers who were helping strugglers beat the odds and achieve. What they found is noteworthy: "Time spent in small-group instruction for reading distinguished the most effective schools from the other schools in the study" (Taylor, 2000).

Time Spent in Reading Instruction by School Effectiveness Level

	Minutes Spent in Small Group	Minutes Spent in Whole Group	Minutes Spent in Independent Reading	Total Minutes in Reading
Most Effective Schools	60	25	28	113
Moderately Effective Schools	36	37	27	90
Least Effective Schools	38	30	19	87

Grouping Patterns and Teacher Effectiveness

	Time Spent in Whole-Group Instruction	Time Spent in Small-Group Instruction
Most Accomplished Teachers	25 minutes/day	48 minutes/day
Moderately Accomplished Teachers	29 minutes/day	39 minutes/day
Least Accomplished Teachers	48 minutes/day	25 minutes/day

> *If kids read—and read and read—books they love, they will succeed.*

Matching Great Text to Readers

We know our students need text that they can read across a range of genres that showcase a variety of text structures. In this way, students will learn how to make critical reading adjustments to accommodate different kinds of texts. The importance of matching just-right books to our resistant readers is well documented:

- Whenever we design an intervention for struggling readers, the single most critical factor that will determine the success of the effort is matching struggling readers with texts they can actually read with a high level of accuracy, fluency, and comprehension" (Allington, 2009).

It's Not Complicated! © 2012 by Phyllis C. Hunter, Scholastic

- Using *appropriately* difficult texts—books that are truly matched to each reader—produced substantive reading growth (O'Connor, et al., 2002).

- Providing lots of opportunities for struggling readers to read texts with high accuracy (99 percent) explained almost all of the success the teachers had in producing accelerated growth (Ehri, et al., 2007).

Walczyk & Griffin-Ross (2007) found that struggling readers benefit from having some say in what they read and how they read it; in other words, they benefit when they are allowed to choose books they want to read and to slow down their reading and implement strategies such as reading out loud, backtracking and rereading, pausing, skipping words they don't know, sounding out, analogizing to a known word, or using context to predict what word might come next.

Guthrie (2004), commenting on the results of two large national and international sets of data examining the relationship between reading engagement and achievement, writes, "Based on this massive sample, this finding suggests the stunning conclusion that engaged reading can overcome traditional barriers to reading achievement, including gender, parental education, and income" (p. 5). If kids read—and read and read—books they love, they will succeed.

Tier 1 Instruction

Once you've matched your struggling readers with appropriate text, your exemplary core instruction aligns perfectly with the goals and targeted support of Tier I intervention:

- Introduce the text to your students, providing background information and pointing out such text features as structure, topics, vocabulary, plot, illustrations, and other graphics.

- Intervene as needed to demonstrate specific comprehension strategies as well as to prompt and reinforce your students' thinking.

- Reinforce effective problem solving of words using the meaning and decoding strategies.

- Demonstrate, reinforce, or prompt the self-correcting of errors that interfere with meaning-making.

- Demonstrate, reinforce, or prompt using punctuation to aid meaning, reading with phrasing, pausing appropriately, stressing the correct words, or using expression.

- Guide a discussion—after your students have read—that probes for deeper meaning and helps to extend their thinking.

- Link reading and discussion to writing as yet another way to extend thinking.

The majority of your vulnerable readers will thrive and succeed with Tier I Intervention. Indeed, Allington notes (2009) that this potent mix of informed, strategic reading instruction in a small-group setting, coupled with engaging text that students can read, is the key to success for most struggling readers.

TIER 2

On the other hand, if your students fail to respond successfully to your Tier 1 intervention, you'll increase and intensify your invention. Aim for five days a week, working within small groups, and provide explicit, scaffolded, targeted intervention that continues to demonstrate, prompt for, and reinforce problem-solving strategies. (This is in addition to your daily core instruction.) With Tier 2 intervention, you will:

- draw attention to the ways in which words work, for example, pointing out first letters, plurals, word endings, consonant clusters, vowel pairs, syllables, and the like.

- watch for opportunities as your students read to teach, prompt, and demonstrate how to take words apart; teach word solving rapidly and efficiently.

- engage your students in word work and help them attend to meaningful word parts such as affixes, base words, root words, homophones, synonyms, and antonyms.

- help your students develop the automatic word recognition and comprehension strategies that enable fluent reading.

- demonstrate, prompt for, and reinforce all the strategies that accelerate proficient reading—comprehension, phonics, and fluency.

TIER 3

Occasionally, despite your best efforts through your Tier 1/core reading program and the intensified intervention of Tier 2, you may still encounter a few at-risk strugglers who need even more extensive invention. Within Tier 3, intense, extensive, one-on-one support, coupled with a wide range of texts your students can read is your best bet for moving kids into successful, proficient reading. You may work one-on-one with the student and engage the services of a literacy specialist or, as needed, you may consider referring your at-risk student for special education testing and services—but this should be your last resort.

What the Research Says About RTI and Supporting Struggling Readers

Oprah once famously declared, "Reading saved my life." Our kids of color can't survive and thrive without on-target reading skills, and the research tells us too many are still not on grade level. Indeed, our poor black youth are falling even further behind, as evident in these tough statistics:

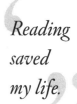

Reading saved my life.

—*Oprah Winfrey*

- 40 percent of black children are born into poverty.
- 85 percent of black children in fourth grade cannot read or do math at grade level, and later almost half of these children drop out of school.
- An African American boy born in 2001 has a one in three chance of going to prison in his lifetime.

Most African American adults believe that half or more of all black children will experience the following events before reaching adulthood:

- profiling based on race from law enforcement
- getting into trouble with the law
- serving time in jail or prison
- being denied important opportunities because of their race
- experiencing crushing unemployment

It's Not Complicated

So what are we waiting for? Time to get on board with RTI. And let's answer this question honestly: If some schools can teach their kids to read at grade level, why can't *all* the schools in a district do it?

RTI accomplishes the following three goals:

- It develops a more valid way of identifying kids of color who are struggling as readers.

- It catches students at risk of failure through early intervention.

- It elevates teachers' professional understanding of effective reading instruction and improves the overall approach to helping students who don't initially "get" reading.

While reading proficiency can't overcome all the challenges our kids of color face, it's clear that without it, they will almost certainly fail. Ultimately, RTI moves us away from a model of failure to one of prevention.

DON'T-MISS RESOURCES

What Really Matters for Struggling Readers: Designing Research-Based Programs

by Richard Allington

This book explains what the research says, why it works, and how to use it to provide intensive, expert reading instruction for all children. Allington aims to help teachers design reading remediation and intervention programs that really work.

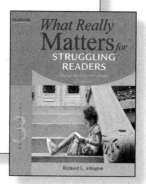

"Everywhere we go and on everything we ride to get there, we're dealing with nonfiction text."

Knowing How to Navigate Nonfiction Is a Survival Skill for Kids

*T*hese days, nonfiction makes the world go round. Practically everything we read on the Internet, for example, is nonfiction. In fact, if you tried to keep track of each time you encountered nonfiction text over the course of a day, you'd go nuts! Nonfiction text is everywhere—inside our homes and outside on the roads we take to get to the shopping center, doctor's office, sports arena, public schools, movie theaters—everywhere we go and on everything we ride to get there, we're dealing with nonfiction text.

Jim Haskins, author of more than a hundred books for adults and young people, explains why he's always preferred nonfiction:

> *I learned to read early and my mother encouraged my love of reading as best she could. There was not a lot of money for books, and the Demopolis (Alabama) Public Library was off-limits to blacks, so some of my earliest reading material was the* World Book Encyclopedia, *which my mother got at the local supermarket—buy a certain dollar amount of groceries, and*

get a volume of the encyclopedia. This is probably one reason why
I prefer nonfiction.

Common Core State Standards and the 21st Century

Fiction used to rule in school—but no more. As we begin our race through the 21st Century, new technical information is doubling every 72 hours (Darling-Hammond 2010). We all understand that we've entered the Knowledge Age, and nonfiction and informational text deserve a prominent place on our classroom library shelves. Plus, if you live in a state that has adopted the Common Core State Standards, then you need to make sure that you are promoting fiction and nonfiction equally—a 50/50 split. The 2009 reading framework of the National Assessment of Education Progress (NAEP) is also nudging us toward nonfiction since, as students move through the grades, they find increasingly more nonfiction on the NAEP assessment. If we follow the NAEP guidelines, by fourth grade, 50 percent of our students' reading material should be nonfiction, 55 percent by eighth grade, and as much as 70 percent across the school day by the time our students reach high school.

> *Fiction used to rule in school—but no more.*

The Common Core State Standards also ask us to help our students develop their "literate capacities"—which means, in part, the ability to *apply* what they know to new life challenges. In today's world, with its deluge of information, focusing on application rather than memorization is wise. Helping our students learn how to use their minds, read critically, synthesize, analyze, and get to the heart of what they need to address should define the instructional focus in our classrooms.

What Is Nonfiction?

Fountas and Pinnell (2006) remind us that "All nonfiction texts have one thing in common: they are based on documentable facts" (p. 172). Mind you, the range within nonfiction is significant; nonfiction text may follow a chronological, narrative structure that traces the unfolding events of a person's life, as in a biography, or appear as a series of sections that categorize specific information. For example, a science text for kids entitled "Teeth Show What Animals Eat" is divided into four sections: Meat Eater, Plant Eater, Meat & Plant Eater, and Fun Dental Facts. And, as is typical of nonfiction, the information is conveyed through both text and graphics that may include photographs, captions, charts, diagrams, and a variety of headings and subheadings. As Fountas & Pinnell (2006) explain, factual texts:

- are organized into sections or categories, rather than the narrative structure of fiction, and marked by headings and subheadings;
- may focus on particular people, topics, or places, but do not typically feature characters or settings;
- present, as needed, an index, table of contents, glossaries, and bibliographies;
- include graphics, such as maps, charts, and diagrams that add meaning;
- illuminate text with realistic illustrations, photographs, and captions;
- feature specialized fonts, such as boldface and italics;
- reflect a range of organizational patterns to provide information to readers, such as description, enumeration, comparison and contrast, cause and effect, chronological sequence, problem/solution, and question/answer—all of which help the reader search, find, and understand specific information;
- showcase factual text that's accurate or scientifically true; readers of informational text enter with the belief that what they are reading accurately represents the facts (p. 184).

Given the different structure and content of a nonfiction text, it's no surprise that a nonfiction text demands a different set of reading strategies. Increasingly, the reading that both we and our students do involves processing highly visual digital texts nonlinearly and selectively (Greenhow, Robelia, & Hughes, 2009).

INFO TEXT: NOTHING BUT THE FACTS!

When it comes to *informational text*, a subcategory of nonfiction, facts rule. Nell Duke defines this factual text as "text written with the primary purpose of conveying information about the natural and social world (typically from someone presumed to be more knowledgeable on the subject to someone presumed to be less so) and having particular text features to accomplish this purpose" (2003, p. 16). Another feature of informational text is the fact that it is often *discontinuous* in nature; that is, unlike sentences and paragraphs inside a narrative text, it may stand alone—not part of a rich meaning network of connected sentences. And it's this discontinuity that may alter the ways in which our students approach, navigate, and comprehend information-rich text.

A sign or one-word caption, for example, is discontinuous text and, at some point, children who are learning to read must figure out how this text operates differently from the connected narrative they typically encounter in picture books. Often discontinuous text is embedded in a visual display, which may feature an array of graphics with varying colors, fonts, and illustrations, all of which provide our students with meaning. Other examples of informational text include:

- Catalogs
- Ads
- How-to Charts
- Menus
- Brochures with maps (or Invitations with maps)
- Web pages
- Games with directions
- Fact books (Guidebooks, Almanacs)
- Magazine articles

SURVIVING THE INFORMATION AGE: WHY WE NEED MORE INFORMATIONAL TEXT IN OUR CLASSROOMS

As our world grows increasingly complex and interconnected, informational text may be the key to academic success. And since the Common Core State Standards are calling for more informational text than ever before, districts around the country are ramping up their use of nonfiction and informational texts (Fertig, 2010). What's more, many students prefer to read informational text. This may be more true than ever, given its abundance, particularly in a digital format, and may also be especially true for boys.

DON'T-MISS RESOURCES

Everyday Literacy

We're finally waking up to an obvious fact: our kids are immersed in a sea of print. Morning, noon, and night, they are following street signs, scanning fast food menus, or downloading their favorite songs from iTunes. Each one of these activities entails a very special kind of reading and text: *info text*—print that conveys information. And now *Everyday Literacy* pulls all that real-life text together for you; you'll find brochures and maps, guidebooks and fact books, magazine articles and games with directions. It's all "Everyday Literacy"— because there's always a reason to read.

Best for Our Boys of Color

Kids love informational text; indeed, it's often the best text for boys. Nell Duke writes, "We found that the boys' reading development finally took off when their teachers provided them with a reading and writing diet rich in informational text—a type of text these boys strongly preferred" (2003, p. 3). In general, we must be vigilant about looking at current research; otherwise, old views might drive instruction. For example, many of us might think that the biggest gender gap we face in education is girls' and boys' achievement in math, but this study and others tell us the biggest gender gap we must close is in reading.

To this end, then, let's make sure that we supply our boys of color with lots of informational texts to read and learn from, including nonfiction books about topics boys are typically interested in (like hobbies or sports), instructional manuals, magazines and newspapers, and, whenever possible, access to websites on topics of interest.

DON'T-MISS RESOURCES

Pam Allyn's Best Books for Boys

by Pam Allyn

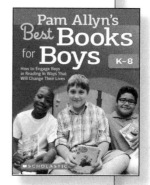

Get all boys reading with this extraordinary guide—chock-full of a wide range of must-read titles organized by interest, age, and development. With this resource in hand, you'll never again struggle to find the right book for even your most reluctant readers. The carefully chosen book selections are accompanied by brief explanations of each book, and a recurring feature, "Talk About It," will help you extend the book through conversation, supporting and enhancing the reading experience. In addition, ready-to-use lessons align with themes and topics of special interest to boys that will motivate and inspire them to read more. Finally, Pam answers your most pressing questions about the challenges for boys as readers and shows how you can maximize environments, routines, and structures to ensure that boys are reading widely and passionately; for use with Grades K-8.

Best for Reluctant Readers

Even struggling readers may prefer and benefit from informational text in ways not possible with narrative. Vulnerable readers are often challenged by limited vocabularies that make processing complex narratives difficult. An infusion of informational text—particularly about topics that stoke our students' interest—may be the easiest way to build the conceptual knowledge and vocabulary base that's essential for comprehension in general. In fact, there may be no better, more efficient way to build world knowledge and an extensive vocabulary than processing lots and lots of informational text. Since such text is written to convey key facts about the natural and social world and often contains a highly specialized vocabulary, it provides a jumpstart to building both a robust vocabulary and wide-ranging conceptual knowledge even for very young children.

The benefits of immersion in informational texts extend to writing development as well. In one study, kindergarten students who simply listened to informational books read aloud incorporated content knowledge, vocabulary, and informational text structures such as diagrams and scientific illustrations in their own writing (Duke & Kays, 1998).

Getting the Most Out of Nonfiction Texts

To help your students get the most out of the nonfiction books they read, you'll want to spend time helping them learn about the unique features and structure of nonfiction books, including, at times, the discontinuity of informational text. You may also want to share the Reading Nonfiction checklist with them, and show them how to use these strategies. That way, each time they immerse themselves in a nonfiction text, they'll have the tools they need to tackle and understand.

What the Research Says About Nonfiction and Text Diversity

Literacy educator and researcher Jeff Wilhelm quotes a young teen who wryly observes, "Teachers ruin reading for nine months and then they try to ruin it for the summer, too." We can avoid destroying reading for our kids of color if we embrace their reading interests and recognize that many *are* engaged in wide reading across a diverse range of mediums, including conventional books and print material, but also much of it digital. This includes:

- social media such as Facebook
- information searches online (Google and Wikipedia)
- video games, gaming manuals and magazines, and video game novels

It's Not Complicated! © 2012 by Phyllis C. Hunter, Scholastic

Reading Nonfiction

Before Reading —

- I think about why I am reading and what information I want to learn.
- I study the book cover and title.
- I read about the author.
- I think about the topic and make connections to what I already know about it.
- I skim the photographs, charts, graphs, maps, and other illustrations and graphics.
- I skim the table of contents and text and pay attention to the headings.

During Reading —

- I stop and check to see if what I have read makes sense.
- I use diagrams, headings, illustrations, and captions to aid my understanding.
- I use the table of contents and index to help me find information.
- I use the glossary to find the meaning of words I don't know.
- I identify confusing words or passages.
- I reread confusing words or passages.
- I ask questions.
- I identify main ideas and supporting details.
- I recognize words that signal transitions and words that signal organizational patterns such as cause and effect.
- I am aware of how the information is organized.
- I make connections to what I already know and determine additional information that I still need to know.
- I visualize or make mental pictures of things not illustrated.
- I take notes if I am writing a report or studying for a test.

After Reading —

- I summarize the text in my own words.
- I reread to find details and confirm facts.
- I look up words that I flagged while reading.
- I look up related information that will help me comprehend the text better.
- I read my notes to make sure they are complete.
- I use the text to support my opinions and ideas.
- I think about what else I want to know.

- texting back and forth (the typical adolescent sends and receives 50 text every day; 15 percent of teens send and receive as many as 200 text a day!)
- TV and movie guides
- programming guides for smart phones, iPads, iTunes, and the like

In other words, our kids may not be reading the traditional novels we recall fondly from our youth, but that doesn't mean they aren't reading. McGill-Franzen & Allington (2008) found that fourth grade children of color preferred "kid culture" books about pop stars, comic book characters, and the like. As they note, "one huge goal of any intervention is to dramatically increase the volume of free voluntary reading by struggling readers. Providing books and magazines that are attractive and interesting to the struggling readers may be the best way to accomplish that goal" (Allington, 2009, p. 158).

Literacy scholar Alfred Tatum, who specializes in investigating the literate lives of young African American adolescent males, suggests in his book, *Teaching Reading to Black Adolescent Males,* that young African American males feel alienated from their school literacy experiences because most school texts don't speak to their life experience. Furthermore, since there are few examples in families, the media, or schools of black males engaging with texts, students don't see literacy as a tool that can transform their world. He argues that it's unlikely that black males will be successful in school if they continue to have fractured literacy experiences. We know these young men can assess and understand complex situations and ideas. The challenge is transferring this skill set to their literacy experiences so they see themselves as part of the classroom discourse.

It's Not Complicated

Literacy educator Jeff Wilhelm makes it easy for us with his quick list of suggestions that will help propel kids toward texts they love to read:

- Give more choice.
- Reward free reading but don't grade it.
- Provide time for reading.
- Value what the kids want to read—trust them.
- Allow kids to stake identity through their reading—through talk, sharing, and response.
- Help students reflect on their reading and what it means to them.
- Focus on meaning, on the edginess, and the emotional charge.

From Wilhelm, J. & Smith, M. (2002). "Reading don't fix no Chevys": Literacy in the lives of young men. Portsmouth, NH: Heinemann.

It's Not Complicated! © 2012 by Phyllis C. Hunter, Scholastic

As Jeff Wilhelm says, "Value what the kids want to read—trust them." All kids have interests and hobbies; invite them to pursue their interests in the reading materials they choose. Goodness knows I can never read enough about my hobby!

DON'T-MISS RESOURCES

Genre: Reading and Writing with Purpose

by Nell K. Duke, Samantha Caughlan, Mary Juzwik, and Nicole Martin

This book is about teaching genre differently—with purpose—in ways that will reinvigorate your teaching. Drawing from theory and research that suggests students learn better and more deeply when learning is contextualized and genuinely motivated, the book presents five guiding principles for teaching genre. Emphasizing purposeful communication, it will guide you through teaching students to read, write, speak, and listen to different real-world genres that inspire and engage them.

"Parents send the best kids they've got to school. If they had better kids to send, they would."

Supporting Families of Color: The Diversity Advantage

*W*hen I was principal of Shepherd Elementary School in Hayward, California, and my superintendant wanted to take my three Reading Recovery-trained teachers and move them to another school, I said, "No way. You're not taking my three most experienced, best-trained teachers; we need them here." And on another note, which may seem unrelated, when my superintendent decided to save money by giving up grounds maintenance and suggested he would no longer mow my school's grounds, I told him to get a crew over to my school pronto. A school in a poor neighborhood with overgrown yards and weeds sends entirely the wrong message to the diverse community we serve: we don't care about the appearance of our school—which really says—*we don't care about your kids.* No way—not under my watch—and not under yours!

Parents, Grandparents, and Caregivers Are Their Child's First Teacher

No one would ever argue that parents don't play a pivotal role in their children's education; parents count, and certainly, the most involved parents often make a huge difference: their children tend to be actively engaged in all aspects of school, turn their homework in on time, and score well on tests, including high-stakes standardized

> *It is time for parents to teach young people early on that in diversity there is beauty and there is strength.*
>
> —*Maya Angelou*

tests. Three cheers for parents! We welcome them to our classrooms and are always delighted when they are able to come. That said, if they don't—and there are many reasons parents don't show, including pinched schedules because they are working multiple jobs, young children at home, and, the most frequent reason, a language barrier—we don't hold it against them, and we don't refuse to provide their children with our full, loving support simply because their parents aren't able to participate in school meetings and events. Today, while we work to hold parents of color responsible for their children's education, let us remember the immigrant parents of bygone days—we didn't demand those parents participate in all school events. I'm just saying: let's keep things in perspective. We welcome parents always, but we don't hold it against them if they're not able to meet with us at school.

And let's keep in mind that this goes both ways. During the first days of school in the fall, I advise all teachers to call the parents or make a home visit. Introduce yourself and say how happy you are to have Abdulla in your class. Say something about what the class will be learning and then sign-off and say good-bye. This makes the first contact with the parent short, sweet, and positive. This action is a deposit of good faith—money in the bank. Even if things go wrong later, the very first contact has been a good one. I haven't met a teacher yet who does not want to meet the family of every student.

> *Reach out to parents from day one. It's a deposit of good faith—money in the bank.*

Making Parents Feel Welcome

Educator Patricia Edwards reminds us that *all* families have strengths; cultural differences are not an unknown to fear but a plus that we should embrace and value. We also need to understand that nearly all parents love their children and want the very best for them. We must never assume anything less. Parents will always be our best partners because no one knows our students better than their parents. Edwards coined the term *differentiated parenting* (2010) to help us understand that we need to provide multiple ways to interact with and support our parents. While all parents want their children to succeed in school, different parents have different needs and challenges; one size does not fit all.

IT'S ALL ABOUT COMMUNICATION

If your parents can't come to you, work hard to go to them: consider making home visits or use the most effective, easiest method of communication; that might be phone

It's Not Complicated! © 2012 by Phyllis C. Hunter, Scholastic

calls, texts, email, tweets, newsletters, a class website that you update frequently, or postcards home. Help your parents understand that you are eager to connect with them at least once a week and then let them know the best ways to reach you, too—before school, during lunch, or after school. In addition to your weekly contact, meet with every parent at least once a year, preferably twice, with follow-up as needed. And to overcome possible language barriers, be sure to include a language translator.

> *Every parent has his or her own story to tell.*
>
> —Judith Vandergrift and Andrea Greene, 1992

One of the best ways to help your parents understand what's going on in your classroom is by sending home folders of student work, ideally every other week or, at least, monthly; invite parents to review the folders and provide a sheet for their comments. In this way, parents will have a better understanding of your program and join you in monitoring their child's progress.

WHAT ARE PARENT STORIES?

Too often, in our efforts to understand our students' home environments, we may ask parents what Pat Edwards calls "one-dimensional questions." For example:

- How many hours per week do you routinely spend reading stories to your child?
- Have you set aside a certain time every day to read to your child?
- Do you encourage your child to read or tell you a story?
- Do you provide books and magazines for your child to read?
- Do you talk and listen to your child?
- Do you and your child visit the library regularly?
- Are you selective about the TV programs your child watches?
- Do you talk about and discuss the programs with your child?

While these questions are important and parents' answers would certainly be revealing, to some parents, particularly those who represent cultural diversity, such a list of questions may come across as an interrogation, raising their defensive levels and adding to their general discomfort around school. Instead of thrusting traditional "school culture" on our parents, what if, first, we invite them to share their culture with us? Imagine what might happen if we were to invite our parents to share their stories with us. In our zeal to connect with parents, too often we fail to consider their personal knowledge or *funds of knowledge* (Moll, et al., 2001) that all students and their parents bring to school. Edwards explains:

Parent "stories" are the narratives gained from open-ended conversations and/or interviews. In these interviews, parents respond to questions designed to provide information about traditional and nontraditional early literacy activities and experiences that have happened in the home. (Edwards, 1999, pp. xxii–xxiii)

Gathering Parent Stories

As Pat Edwards reminds us, parent stories provide teachers with the opportunity to gain a deeper understanding of the "human side" of families and children. This might include why children behave as they do, how they like to learn and communicate, some of the challenges parents are coping with at home, and how these challenges might influence their children's attitudes and behavior in school (Edwards, et al., 1999, p. xviii).

> *School may have the official mission to bring literacy to students, but it is much more accurate to say that students bring literacy—or rather literacies—to school. Home literacy comes embedded in complex social and emotional meanings that need to be acknowledged and built upon, not ignored or dismantled, in school.*
>
> —Brandt, 1985, p. 135

Equally important, parent stories offer a way out of the "blame game." Once we really understand our children's families, we're less likely to blame them for the challenges we might face connecting with their kids at school and offering the full support we're striving to deliver. Once we achieve a deeper understanding of every student and family in our care, we'll be in a much better position to provide instruction that's shaped to fit the range of needs always present in every classroom (Edwards, et al., 1999, p. xxiv) Here's a new way to listen to parents and learn from them:

- Can you describe something about your home learning environment that you feel might be different from the learning environment of the school?

- Can you describe something about your home learning environment that you would like the school to build upon because you feel that it might enhance your child's learning potential at school?

- Is there something about your child that might not be obvious to the teacher, but might positively or negatively affect his or her performance in school? If so, what would that something be?

It's Not Complicated! © 2012 by Phyllis C. Hunter, Scholastic

SUPPORTING THEIR CHILD AT HOME

Finally, once you establish a bond of mutual respect and understanding with the parents of your students, you'll be in a better position to offer them tips they can implement at home to support their children's developing reading and writing.

- Recognize that a love of reading might well be your most important educational goal for your children.

- Show you value reading by reading in front of children and talking about what you're reading, and, depending on what you're reading, how valuable or enjoyable you find the text. Demonstrate all the different reasons you read every day!

- Don't worry about scheduling a specific time for your children to read. If they love reading, any time is a good time.

- Don't be concerned about making your children read only "quality literary books"—the more important goal is that they read deeply and widely in text of all types—and that includes digital text, too, such as text messages, Web pages, video game directions, and the like.

- Search out books your children will like. Get familiar with their reading tastes and make a point of taking them to the public library as often as you can (to that end, make sure they have library cards).

- Be careful that you don't schedule so many activities for your children that they have little time to read (this includes babysitting siblings, sports, chores—and, especially, monitor TV viewing).

- Make sure that your children can some day enjoy classics by not pushing them too early.

- Don't worry if your kids have periods in their lives when they don't demonstrate avid reading.

- If you have older children who already dislike reading, don't blame yourself.

- Never give up on your children. No matter how old they are, they can be brought to a love of books. Just keep encouraging them!

> *You take a black man who doesn't have a job, but you say to him, 'Look, you can make a difference in your child's life, just by reading to him for 30 minutes a day.'*
>
> —*Walter Dean Myers, Award-winning author, Ambassador of Children's Literature, 2012*

It may be that our schools need to expand the vision of their mission—as Geoffrey Canada has done in the Harlem Children's Zone—and work cooperatively with a range of community service providers. In this way, the school becomes the focal point of care the entire community needs. And everyone in the community—teachers, administrators, parents, service providers—assume an all-hands-on-deck stance and work together to provide an exemplary academic experience for the community's children.

What the Research Says About Supporting Families

Children's books in the home closes the black-white gap in kindergarten. Fryer and Levitt (2004) examined reading and math test scores in kindergarten and first grade using data from the Early Childhood Longitudinal Study (about 1,000 schools). They focused on the so-called achievement gap between black and white children.

- For reading, the difference between black and white children at the start of kindergarten was .40 (where 0 = mean, sd = 1). Thus, black children scored 40 percent of one standard deviation below white children.

- When Fryer and Levitt controlled for SES, (parents' education, parent occupation, household income), the gap dropped to .134.

- When they controlled for SES and number of children's books in the home, the gap dropped to nearly zero—.006.

- This is a major result: social class and the presence of children's books even the playing field. As Fryer and Levitt note, "including number of books completely eliminates the gap in reading" (p. 452).

Levitt controlled for more predictors, including age at kindergarten, birth weight, mother's age at the time her first child was born, the characteristics of neighborhood, mother's work status, preschool program participation, parental involvement in child's life, family size and family structure, the difference was .093. Black children did slightly better.

So why do low-income white students typically have higher mean scores on standardized tests than middle-income African Americans? And, in a similar vein, why do middle-income white students outscore upper-income African American students? This data from the National Longitudinal Survey of Youth (NLSY) and reported in Jairrels (2009) seems to offer a possible explanation. African American families may not have books in their home nor do they have a tradition of reading aloud to their children; as a result, their kids may not be getting the birth-to-five literacy jumpstart that white middle class kids typically get. Note: the researchers use the terms "poor" and "nonpoor" to refer to the socioeconomic status of the families.

Children's Ages: Birth to Two Years, Eleven Months

Percentage Reporting Reading at Least Three Times a Week to Daily

White	66.7 of nonpoor mothers	44.9 of poor mothers
African American	43.8 of nonpoor mothers	31.7 of poor mothers

Children's Ages: Birth to Two Years, Eleven Months

Percentage Reporting Ten or More Books in the Home

White	63 of nonpoor mothers	41.8 of poor mothers
African American	33 of nonpoor mothers	19.7 of poor mothers

Children's Ages: Three to Five Years, Eleven Months

Percentage Reporting Reading at Least Three Times a Week to Daily

White	71.4 of nonpoor mothers	55.4 of poor mothers
African American	45 of nonpoor mothers	33.3 of poor mothers

Children's Ages: Three to Five Years, Eleven Months

Percentage Reporting Ten or More Books in the Home

White	93.4 of nonpoor mothers	74.6 of poor mothers
African American	67.8 of nonpoor mothers	39.9 of poor mothers

Children's Ages: Six to Nine Years, Eleven Months

Percentage Reporting Reading at Least Three Times a Week to Daily

White	45.2 of nonpoor mothers	35.7 of poor mothers
African American	30.3 of nonpoor mothers	28 of poor mothers

Children's Ages: Six to Nine Years, Eleven Months

Percentage Reporting Ten or More Books in the Home

White	94.7 of nonpoor mothers	80.3 of poor mothers
African American	75.3 of nonpoor mothers	47.8 of poor mothers

Children's Ages: Ten to Fourteen Years, Eleven months

Percentage Reporting Ten or More Books in the Home

White	73.5 of nonpoor mothers	50.9 of poor mothers
African American	41.6 of nonpoor mothers	26.1 of poor mothers

It's Not Complicated

Time is more important than money. You can get more money, but you can't get more time. We don't have forever to get this done! Take a hard look at the fabulous parent brochure Dr. Alfred Tatum and University of Illinois colleagues have put together for the Tavis Smiley Foundation.

Parents: Every Child's First Teacher
Home Education Strategies
From Birth Through High School

This fabulous guide from the Tavis Smiley Foundation—developed by the University of Illinois, Chicago Reading Clinic—features everything you need to know to support your child from the moment of birth to the day you deliver him or her to college. Do not miss!

Tapping the Potential of Parents:
A Strategic Guide to Building Student
Achievement Through Family Involvement

by Patricia A. Edwards

School-home communication and cooperation are lifelines that will improve the academic achievement of all children regardless of race or economic status, cultural or linguistic background. This breakthrough book features concrete strategies that foster strong family-school partnerships which, in turn, help guarantee student success. The strategies, which enable teachers to interact with diverse families, include class and school demographic profiles, parenting contracts, parent vision statements, and parent informant literacy groups.

Tell your kids that they are excellent test takers—and watch them take off.

Helping Our Kids Means Being Smart About the Use of Data

*W*hen I was a reading manager, people were saying, "all the black kids are not doing well." But when I drilled down into the data, I discovered that the African American boys were not doing as well as they should be. The girls, on the other hand, were so we couldn't make sweeping generalizations and claim that all African American kids were falling behind.

Focus on What Kids *Can* Do

In his book *The Essential 55,* Harlem middle school teacher Ron Clark tells the story of Arlis, who was a "solid D" student. One day, when they were reading *The Lion, the Witch, and the Wardrobe*, Ron asked the class to predict what was going to happen in the next chapter. Arlis raised his hand and said, "I think there's going to be an older spell that is good that is going to cancel out the bad one." He was absolutely right and Ron made a big deal of it:

I sure milked that for all it was worth. I pointed out to all the kids how brilliant his prediction was and how proud of him I was for figuring that out. Then I asked a few of my colleagues to do me a favor and mention to Arlis that they had heard he made some really good observations about the novel we were reading. I called his mom and told her I was proud of Arlis for paying attention during reading and that he was doing an excellent job of participating in class. (188–189)

From that day forward, no matter how far out Arlis' comments might be, Ron always found a way to comment in a positive way. And all that positive praise eventually paid off. By the end of the year, Arlis had become one of Ron's top reading students. Receiving Ron's praise boosted Arlis' self-confidence, he began to believe that he was an exceptional student, and, in the process, he became one.

> *Use praise liberally. Our children must feel our love.*

As we consider how best to assess our students, let's recognize that effective assessment not only examines students' abilities, skills, and strategies, but also their motivations, attitudes, and cultural traditions. For this reason, we always want to use multiple sources to gather our assessment data so we can make thoughtful, informed decisions about our students' instructional needs. And it's essential that we remain flexible. The snapshot we capture of one student's learning one day might look very different a month later as that student continues to grow and develop through a network of learning experiences. For this reason, at all costs, we want to avoid pigeonholing our students by ability. We must remain open to the promise of their growth and development. Every classroom has an Arlis—or four or five; how can you use your assessment data to identify these kids' strengths and build on them?

How Do We Know Our Kids Are Making Progress?

When it comes to evaluating our kids, we all need to pay attention. Parents need to pay attention to assessments that come home—is your child on grade level? Teachers need to pay attention to reading assessments and use that data to inform their instruction, and administrators need to use the data to determine what's working in their school and what's not.

The most effective feedback comes from continuous assessment, and ideally, when it's offered, it is detailed, specific, and immediate. Vague feedback offered days after kids

It's Not Complicated! © 2012 by Phyllis C. Hunter, Scholastic

have written a paper or performed in Reader's Theater or participated in a class discussion is of little value. Writing *good* on a student's paper without spelling out *why* it's good doesn't help a student understand the details of her accomplishment so that she can repeat and even exceed it. Kids need immediate information: specifically, in detail, what did they do that works, and why. And what did they do that didn't work as well; what do they need to improve and why.

The key to assessment is the word itself. It comes from the Latin verb *assidere, to sit beside* (Lane, 2008). As we think about how to determine whether our students are becoming successful readers, consider that our most accurate and revealing information might well arise from sitting beside our students and asking just a few essential questions:

- Do our students read—not just when they are assigned reading, but on their own time as well?

- Do they have favorite topics, genres, authors?

- Do they talk about books with others? Can they explain why they love their current book?

- Do they know the next book(s) they plan to read?

If we can answer *yes* to these questions and other similar ones, then we know our students are becoming *engaged readers*—ultimately our best indicator that they are developing the skills, strategies, and insights they need to support proficient reading. As the saying goes, a student just needs to get lost once in a good book to forever fall in love with reading. She will then spend the rest of her life seeking that glorious experience again and again.

> *Keep your data current. Some data is so old the kids have left the school.*

Process and Product, Formative and Summative

Peter Afflerbach (2008) reminds us that reading assessment necessarily means that we are making inferences about our students' growth and development; to this end, we want to focus on both the process and product of their reading development.

PROCESS-BASED, FORMATIVE ASSESSMENT

Typically, process-based formative assessments center on students' skills, strategies, and work as they unfold; in other words, we pay attention to the skills and strategies that enable our students to construct meaning from text:

- decoding words
- accessing prior knowledge
- figuring out the meaning of new vocabulary words
- reading fluently
- monitoring their own comprehension processes

We use formative assessments such as reading inventories or running records as we interact with our students—as the process of teaching and learning unfolds. In this way, we can identify the teachable moments when we can step in with just-right targeted instruction that will help students take their next developmental leap. Instruction delivered at the point of need is always more effective than assigned exercises that have nothing to do with our students' needs.

Examples of Formative Assessment

Since the goal of formative assessment is to glean what students know and don't know in order to adjust our instructional strategies and techniques, our own classroom observations play a key role, as do whole-class and small-group discussions. Every time we engage our students in conversation, we gain a window into their evolving understandings. And we can zero in on their understanding by asking open-ended, thoughtful questions that produce expansive answers:

- Invite students to discuss their thinking about a question or topic in pairs or small groups; ask a representative to share the thinking with the larger group (also known as a think-pair-share).
- Present several possible answers to a question; ask students to vote on them and explain their choices.
- Ask all students to write down an answer; read aloud a selected few.

You might also assess students' understanding in the following ways:

- Have students write their understanding of vocabulary or concepts before and after instruction.
- Ask students to summarize the main ideas they've taken away from a lecture, discussion, or assigned reading.
- Interview students individually or in groups about their thinking as they discuss the text.
- Assign brief in-class writing assignments—you can use reading journal

It's Not Complicated! © 2012 by Phyllis C. Hunter, Scholastic

entries, a student letter-writing exchange, and similar opportunities to capture in writing students' thoughts about their reading.

- And again: Discuss, discuss, discuss! There is power in discussion for *all* ages.

PRODUCT-SUMMATIVE ASSESSMENT

In contrast, product-based summative assessments focus on what students produce as a result of reading. With such national attention on standardized tests, we need to be careful that we don't overemphasize product assessment to the exclusion of process. What are product-summative assessments? Think benchmark exams, standardized tests, and lists of questions about students' comprehension of particular texts that are then scored to produce quantitative data. Ultimately, a single score tells us little about the student's overarching ability; in fact, it's a bit like the score of a basketball game. The score tells us which team won the game but we don't know exactly how they pulled it off. Was it a lucky break because the losing team was off their game and played poorly, or did the winning team play so strategically and brilliantly that they simply overwhelmed the other team and ultimately won the day? As Peter Afflerbach reminds us, single-score, product-based exams are limited:

> *Summative assessment is important, as it helps us understand whether students have reached grade-level benchmarks, unit and lesson goals, and standards in the classrooms, districts, and states. However, summative assessment is, by its nature, an after-the-fact of teaching events. We do not have as rich an opportunity with summative assessment to inform instruction and to address students' individual needs as they are developing.* (p. 273)

> *Teach to the test— why wouldn't you if everything is riding on it?— but do not narrow your curriculum to test prep only.*

Clearly, our assessment goal should be *balance*—a happy medium between our teacher questions and observations of formative assessments, on one hand, and the quantifiable data of summative assessments on the other.

Self-Assessment

Let's not forget to ask our students to evaluate themselves. How do they think they are doing? What's working for them? What's not? The goal is to help our kids learn how to monitor their own reading process. We want our students to understand that reading should always sound like language and make sense and, if it doesn't, they should have a range of fix-it strategies they can use to recover meaning. Indeed, Pressley & Afflerbach (1995) regard the ability to monitor one's own reading as the hallmark of successful reading.

Research has shown that engaging students in a three-step self-assessment cycle typically leads to the greatest opportunities for growth. Students must:

- recognize the learning objectives; what's the goal of each reading lesson?

- understand the assessment criteria and standards used to evaluate their progress

- have opportunities to reflect on their work; what is working well for them? What needs improvement?

It's Not Complicated! © 2012 by Phyllis C. Hunter, Scholastic

Students who participate in this three-step cycle ultimately show greater improvement than those who do not understand the goal of each lesson—and how they will be evaluated and why it all matters.

DEMONSTRATE AND GUIDE

The best way to help students learn how to pay attention and monitor their own reading is relatively simple: offer frequent demonstrations of your own monitoring and provide tools that scaffold. For example, consider this checklist created by a primary teacher:

_____ I check to see if what I read makes sense.

_____ I remind myself why I am reading.

_____ I focus on the goal of my reading while I read.

_____ I check to see if I can summarize sentences and paragraphs.

_____ If reading gets hard, I ask myself if there are any problems.

_____ I try to identify the problem.

_____ I try to fix the problem.

_____ When the problem is fixed, I get back to my reading, making sure I understand what I've read so far.

Tell your kids that they are very good test takers—say it often so they will begin to believe you and act on it.

If we teachers run through this checklist ourselves several times, thinking aloud as we generate answers, our students will quickly get the hang of how it works. What's more, a checklist like this is scalable. We can up the ante and add additional questions that reflect specific instructional goals. For example, if we want to focus on our students' nonfiction critical reading skills, we might add such questions as these:

_____ I check the text to see if the author provides evidence to support claims.

_____ I compare the information in the text with what I already know about the topic. (Afflerbach, p. 275)

What the Research Says About Assessment

Our students of color have not been served well by traditional school assessment. We have been hit hard by something known as *disproportionality*; in other words, when students' representation in special education programs or specific special education categories exceeds their proportional enrollment in a school's general population, something is not right and a red flag should go up. Let's dig into these disturbing numbers:

- African American students account for only 14.8 percent of the general population of 6-to-21-year-old students, but they make up 20 percent of the special education population across all disabilities (Losen & Orfield, 2002).

- African American kids are 2.41 times more likely than white students to be identified as having mental retardation.

- African American kids are 1.13 times more likely to be labeled as learning disabled.

- African American kids are 1.68 times as likely to be found to have an emotional or behavioral disorder (Klingner, et al., 2005).

Those of us on the frontlines know that these diagnoses are often made by school personnel, too often relying on a subjective referral and an eligibility determination process that varies from district to district and from school to school. Either way, African American students still experience fewer positive outcomes than their white peers.

DON'T-MISS RESOURCES

The Other Wes Moore

by Wes Moore

Two kids with the same name growing up in the same decaying city. One grew up to be a Rhodes Scholar, decorated combat veteran, White House fellow, and business leader. The other is serving a life sentence for felony murder. Here is the story of two boys and the journey of a generation.

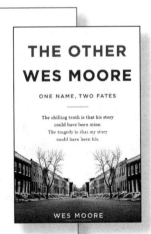

THE OTHER WES MOORE

ONE NAME, TWO FATES

The chilling truth is that his story could have been mine. The tragedy is that my story could have been his.

WES MOORE

Smart Assessment:
Five Ways to Know What Your Kids Know

Let's get smart about measuring what our kids know. Here are five assessment strategies from TeacherVision (see: www.teachervision.fen.com) that ask your kids to get smart and apply their knowledge and skills to real world tasks or performance activities.

1. Performance Assessment

You can ask your students to work collaboratively and to apply skills and concepts to solve complex problems. They might engage in such short-term and long-term activities as:

- writing, revising, and presenting a report to the class
- conducting a week-long science experiment and analyzing the results
- working with a team to prepare a position in a classroom debate

2. Short Investigations

Kick off a short investigation with a stimulus such as a math problem, political cartoon, map, or excerpt from a primary source—then ask kids to interpret, describe, calculate, explain, or predict.

3. Open-Response Questions

Open-response questions, like short investigations, present students with a stimulus and ask them to respond. Responses include:

- a brief written or oral answer
- a mathematical solution
- a drawing
- a diagram, chart, or graph
- a student-designed response

4. Portfolios

A portfolio documents learning over time so kids learn how to self-evaluate, edit, and revise. A student portfolio might include:

- journal entries and reflective writing

~ continued on next page

continued ~

- peer reviews
- artwork, diagrams, charts, and graphs
- group reports
- student notes and outlines
- rough drafts and polished writing

5. Self-Assessment

Invite your students to evaluate their own participation, process, and products and ask:

- What was the most difficult part of this project for you?
- What do you think you should do next?
- If you could do this task again, what would you do differently?
- What did you learn from this project?

Smart assessment will tell you far more about what your students know than a paper-and-pencil, multiple-choice test. Try it in your classroom! ("Authentic Assessment Overview." TeacherVision. Pearson.)

American students who are placed in special education programs are more likely to be characterized by segregated special education placements, limited access to the general education classroom and to peers without disabilities, high dropout rates, low academic performance, and substandard or watered-down curricula (Ferri & Connor, 2005).

And it doesn't end well—after African American students exit special education, most commonly by dropping out or receiving a certificate of attendance, they find themselves swept up in high unemployment rates, lack of preparation for the workforce, and difficulty in gaining access to postsecondary education (Chamberlain, 2005). It's pretty clear that we need urgent research to separate out and identify the connections between race, economic status, disproportionality, and assessment that work against our children.

It's Not Complicated! © 2012 by Phyllis C. Hunter, Scholastic

It's Not Complicated

My Drew was in the gifted program, but I was an educator; I knew what to look for and how to advocate for him. Most parents of color don't even realize a gifted program for their kids might be an option. At last, in districts around the country, school officials are beginning to take notice at the racial disparity of their gifted programs. For example, in Alexandria, Virginia, while 65 percent of its 12,000 elementary and middle school students are children of color (African American and Hispanic) only 28 percent are in the gifted program (Sieff, 2011). This isn't right, and it's about time that districts are taking a hard look at the racial inequality of their gifted programs. ["Washington-area schools confront the 'gifted gap'" Kevin Sieff, *Washington Post*: November 6, 2011] We've got to be smart about our data. Let's use it to promote our kids' success . . . not tear them down.

Believe in yourself—that's the first key to college our kids need.

We Must Help All Kids of Color Believe They Will Go to College

We need to move from a dream to a plan. Even if Martin Luther King, Jr., were here today, he'd say, okay, the dream was nice, but now we need a plan.

William's Story

As a principal in Hayward, California, I never left school before nine o'clock at night because of the tremendous workload. Shepherd Elementary was not an "A school" when I was named its principal; indeed, it was one of the toughest schools in the district. Drug dealing often went on at the south corner where my students crossed to enter to the playground located on our campus. One evening, William was waiting in my office for his mother to pick him up. I needed to speak to her about a fire alarm that happened to go off unexpectedly just as William passed it in the hall. As we waited, I worked on a mountain of paperwork at my desk. Nine-year-old William was obviously bored and started twisting and turning in his seat. When I asked what was wrong with the book he wasn't reading, he asked me a question: "Do you own this school?"

I smiled and said, "No, it belongs to the public, the city, and the district."

He then inquired, "Do you own all these books in this office?"

I said, "Yes, most of them but some belong to the school." Looking at the window William then asked if that was my Cadillac he saw parked outside.

I replied, "Yes."

He then said, "You always look like you just came from the cleaners. How do you get all those clothes? How do you get all this stuff? How did you become a principal?"

I gave him the blow-by-blow description starting with getting a high school diploma, going on to college, and getting an even higher degree and diploma called a Master of Science. He looked me square in the eye and said, "I'm going to get me some of them."

I said, "What? Nice clothes and a car?"

He said, "No, Mrs. Hunter, I'm gonna get me some of those diplomas!"

Many students don't know how education works. They don't know anyone who has obtained an education and had it work for them. That is why we must make it real. Talk it up, expect that they will go to college, explain the procedure, the steps to take, and let them know the benefits.

Help Kids Believe in Themselves

Before our kids are in sixth grade, they need to know what college is, how it works, and why they should want to go.

Rod Paige, the first African American Secretary of Education, told me this story. The Pinnacle Society, an African American men's organization was honoring one of their own (a federal judge) at the Houston Athletic Club. It was a pretty ritzy event, and the kinds of cars being parked outside reflected the wealth of the participants: Mercedes, Bentley, Lexus—all the luxury makes and even a few limos. All the elite Black Male Who's Who of Houston Society were in attendance. Dr. Paige said he wondered how this had come to happen as many of these men's parents were not wealthy—but in one generation they had acquired status and amassed wealth. It occurred to Dr. Paige that what these men did have were degrees, diplomas. They were doctors, lawyers, professors, astronauts, scientists, and college-educated businessmen. The earning of a diploma had made a world of difference between them and the black attendants who parked their cars.

Guiding our kids of color on a trajectory toward college begins with helping them believe in themselves. We must help each one develop the needed self-confidence: *I am worthy of a college education; I have what it takes to apply to college, win entry, and graduate.* To that end, our kids have got to hit the ground running—they need a

It's Not Complicated! © 2012 by Phyllis C. Hunter, Scholastic

complex mix of self-efficacy, hard work and determination, and targeted support from those who know and love them best.

Let's take a look at *self-efficacy* or believing that you have the ability to succeed. For some, that might simply mean not sabotaging their own best interests and opportunities for academic success. In his provocative book, *Losing the Race: Self-Sabotage in Black America*, linguist and political commentator John McWhorter addresses the self-sabotaging phenomenon of not wanting to "act white":

> *I've noted that it is hard to miss an almost alarming pride in disengagement from learning among many black students, arising more from a sense of cultural identity than problems with confidence and stereotype threat . . . and this issue of attitude is borne out by studies; Lawrence Steinberg found, for example, that across nine high schools of various racial compositions and levels of quality, black and Latino students spent less time on homework, cut class more often, and reported zoning out in class much more than Asian and white students.* (p. 130)

"Acting white" has become part of the national consciousness. What does it mean exactly? Roland Fryer, Harvard Professor of Economics, defines the phrase as "a set of social interactions in which minority adolescents who get good grades in school enjoy less social popularity than white students who do well academically" (2006, p. 53). In other words, kids of color who care about school and work hard to do well may be viewed as snobs and shunned by their peers. Obviously, to reject attitudes and behaviors associated with academic success is an immense challenge for the African American and Latino communities. *All* kids should aspire to academic success.

Television, Video Games, and Other Distractions

While "acting white" refers to a set of behaviors and attitudes associated with academic success—caring about your studies, staying organized and meeting deadlines, and allotting the focused time needed to study—zoning out in front of the tube for hours every day is the opposite of what's needed to chart a path to

> *I was teased if I brought my books home. I would take a paper bag to the library and put the books in the bag and bring them home. I felt a little ashamed, having books.*
>
> — Walter Dean Myers, Award-winning author, Ambassador of Children's Literature

> *As a young black man, I can't even recall how many times I heard "nerd" or "geek" or "college boy" or "You sound like a white boy" used as an insult. It's not about "white," it's about education and power. They didn't want me to have either.*
>
> —James, a writer quoted in Tom Burrell, 2010

college. Unfortunately, today's young people devote an astonishing number of hours to television, video games, and social media.

From the Center of Media and Human Development, Northwestern University (2011) comes the first national study to focus exclusively on children's media use by race and ethnicity. It analyzed race data from a 2010 study on media use among 2,000 eight to 18-year-olds and compared it to another 2006 study on another 2,000 children from birth to six years old. Again, we see a divide between white kids and kids of color, a difference that may well serve to undermine the best shot our kids of color have at getting good grades, solid test scores, and entry to college.

- Children of color spent 3 hours and 7 minutes per day watching TV, playing games, and listening to music on their mobiles—about 1.5 hours more each day than white kids.

- Black and Hispanic children watch more than three hours of TV every day, while whites and Asians watch more than two hours.

- Black and Hispanic youth are more likely to have TV sets in their bedrooms–84 percent of blacks, 77 percent of Hispanics, compared to 64 percent of whites and Asians.

- Black children under six are twice as likely to have a TV in their bedroom as whites, and more than twice as likely to go to sleep with the TV on.

- 78 percent of blacks, 67 percent of Hispanics, 58 percent of whites, and 55 percent of Asians eight to 18 years old say the TV is "usually" on during home meals.

Researchers claim that our diverse students spend more than half their day consuming media content, a rate that's four and a half hours greater than their white counterparts. "Traditional television watching is by far the most popular activity among kids, with black and Hispanic youngsters watching more than three hours a day—but this figure doubles to almost six hours when TiVo, DVDs, and mobile and online viewing are taken into account."

Imagine if all these hours devoted to digital media became time spent inside books. An extra three hours a day of reading extended text would yield tremendous positive benefits. However, the failure to achieve and thrive isn't all on our students' shoulders, and their adolescent need to cleave together or partake in the thrill of technology. We as parents, teachers, administrators—as well as politicians and policy makers—also bear responsibility.

It's Not Complicated! © 2012 by Phyllis C. Hunter, Scholastic

Expect More, Fight for More

It's always easy to blame the kids and their families for lack of effort, poor child rearing, and a "culture of poverty" in which those who are trapped in that culture live with feelings of hopelessness, inferiority, and a grim acceptance of their fate. But Stanford University Professor Linda Darling-Hammond points to another culprit: *inequality.* Poor children of color have limited access to quality school resources, engaging curriculum and instruction, thoughtful assessments, and, most important, access to professionally credentialed, knowledgeable teachers.

Educational outcomes for students of color are much more a function of their unequal access to key educational resources, including skilled teachers and a high-quality curriculum, than they are a function of race. These disparities reinforce the wide inequalities in income among families, with the most resources being spent on children from the wealthiest communities and the fewest on the children of the poor, especially in high-minority communities (2010, p. 300).

The gap between high-spending districts that serve predominantly white, well-to-do students and low-spending districts that serve our kids of color is well documented and scandalous. Is it any wonder our students of color often attend school in dilapidated buildings with inadequate books and equipment and poorly trained teachers often without teaching credentials? Darling-Hammond writes, " By every measure of qualification—certification, subject matter background, pedagogical training, selectivity of college attended, test scores, or experience—less-qualified teachers were found in schools serving greater numbers of low-income and minority students" (p. 303). And we know beyond dispute that highly-qualified teachers make all the difference. Control socioeconomic status and assign black students to equally qualified teachers and guess what happens: the gap between black and white test scores closes.

We also need to consider institutionalized school practices that ultimately undermine the ability of our students of color to get themselves on a college path. One of the most harmful, of course, is academic tracking. It's no surprise that most of the lower track courses are filled with students of color. And from a brand new research study by researchers Gloria Rodriguez and Lisbeth Cruz, we learn of the egregious setback English Language Learners endure as the result of tracking:

> *One feature of public schools that is particularly associated with the under preparation of English Language Learners for college is academic tracking and the resulting within-school segregation of ELLs . . . For secondary ELLs, the track placement decision carries implications not*

only for access to supports for English language acquisition but also for access to college-required academic coursework.

As the researchers note, "the pathway to college for English learning students is diverted by the limited capacity and resultant sorting processes of schools" (2011, p. 4).

What can we do to fight back and make sure all our kids of color take pride in their ability and cultural backgrounds, view themselves as college material, and have the academic support they need—quality teachers, access to books and other resources, and all the benefits of a fine, well-maintained, fully-functioning school so they have an honest shot at college?

BEGIN WITH BOOKS: CREATE A LITERATE CULTURE IN YOUR HOME, SCHOOL, AND COMMUNITY

By now you know: I'm all about books. I always return to books. I know the power of books and reading to change lives. And it's not just a hunch based on my experience. We've got hard research that shows it's true.

A comprehensive study led by the University of Nevada sociologist M. D. R. Evans examined statistics from 27 nations and found that just the mere presence of books in the home can elevate a child's chance for academic success; for example, a robust home library of 500 titles or more is the equivalent of having two college educated parents and "propels a child 3.2 years further in education, on average, than would growing up in a similar home with few or no books." And even 20 books in the home can give a child an academic boost. As educators, of course, we understand it's not the books as physical objects, but the "literate culture" they inspire that makes the difference.

> *Evans and her colleagues contend the number of books at home is an excellent reflection of a family's "scholarly culture," which they describe as a "way of life in homes where books are numerous, esteemed, read and enjoyed." An early immersion in such a culture "provides skills and competencies that are useful in school," and/or engenders "a preference for and enjoyment of books and reading that makes schooling congenial, or enjoyable," they conclude. So mom and dad don't have to be scholars themselves; they just have to read and respect books, and pass that love of reading down to their children.* (Jacobs, 2010)

Every day, find a way to nurture your students as readers—find a just-right book for Tony, slip the next book in a series to Esmeralda, invite Tia to accompany you the next

It's Not Complicated! © 2012 by Phyllis C. Hunter, Scholastic

time you make a trip to the public library to fill up with books for the classroom. Every day, these seemingly small gestures add up to create a richly literate reading life.

Consider conducting a "literacy check" of your classroom; ask the kids to draw up the data points: What should count? The numbers of books in the classroom library? How often the books are checked out? How often the books go home? How frequently kids engage in "literary conversations" with their peers? How many kids claim a favorite author? How many books kids read every school year? (The students in middle school teacher's Nancie Atwell's class typically read 40-plus a year.) How many kids can talk about their reading plans for the summer? Do they leave school with a Summer Reading List in hand? Gather this data and other data points like it and see what's needed to boost the literate index of your classroom.

And while we don't want kids to read simply because they are trying to rack up more points than anyone, you might still lure kids to books by sharing this *aim-high-to-achieve-big* information from a study conducted more than 25 years ago by William Nagy and Richard Anderson (1984). They found that:

- the *average* student read about 1,000,000 words a year (to give you a sense of one million words: all seven Harry Potter books = more than 1.8 million words)
- *avid* middle grade readers consumed more than 10,000,000 words per year!

And this difference accounted for the noteworthy differences in their achievement. The avid readers were far better readers, writers, and spellers—and had better control of grammar—than their peers who didn't read as much.

PARENTS, YOU CAN MAKE A DIFFERENCE!

Veda Jairrels is a Professor of Exceptional Education at Clark Atlanta University. She holds master's and doctoral degrees in special education from Teachers College at Columbia University and a law degree from Indiana University. The title of her 2009 book is *African Americans and Standardized Tests: The Real Reason for Low Test Scores.* She notes that as a group, African American students usually (not always) score the lowest on standardized tests that focus on verbal (reading) ability. Why? Dr. Jairrels points to a lack of "long-term voluntary reading." Her message is direct and to the point:

> *Many African American parents do not understand the amount of reading their children must do in order to maximize their scores on standardized tests. They know that reading is important, but they do not know how important and critical it is for improving performance on standardized tests.* (viii)

Whether we agree with the tests or not, they are here and almost certainly will remain a part of our children's educational experience for years to come. And we all recognize that they are used as gatekeepers. Those who score high are able to access the best universities, scholarships—and beyond, and have a better shot at professional, high paying jobs. Those who don't do well on the SAT may find doors closed to higher education and meaningful work. It's not fair nor a smart way to function as a society but, for the time being, it's the way it is and we ignore it at our peril.

What's the secret to scoring high on the SAT and succeeding academically? Jairrels answers: *reading.* Backed by research and drawing from an African American legacy framed by Frederick Douglass among many others, who faced beatings as he sought every opportunity to learn how to read, Jairrels builds a convincing case for reading as transcendence. She notes that until at least the 1960s in the South, generations of African Americans were denied easy access to schools, libraries, books, and reading. Recounting the struggles her family and other poor African Americans endured just to get a rudimentary education, she writes:

> *My parents, grandparents, great-grandparents, etc., had little or no access to books. . . . From West Africa to America, conditions did not allow for the development of a familial reading habit to be passed down from generation to generation. A conscious and concerted effort was made to keep African Americans as uneducated as possible. Consequently, "long-term voluntary reading" (Marx, p. B10, 2002) is not widespread throughout our culture, and many may be unaware of its power. We were denied access because of racism, and the effects of decades of denial have manifested in low scores on standardized tests. Now, for those of us with at least access to libraries (Krashen, 2006), we have the power to increase our scores, if we increase our reading.* (p. 17)

WHAT YOU CAN DO/MUST DO AS A PARENT

You love your children. You want the best for them. What can you do? Create a literacy-rich home environment. Here's a checklist for you to follow; take a tour of your home and see how many you can check off—and add the ones you're not yet doing.

- Do we have lots of print in our home—and do we talk about it? The print might include magazines, books, newspapers, and environmental print of all kinds—on food packaging, appliances, on TV, and so forth.

- Do I provide a variety of types of books, such as storybooks, ABC and rhyming books, informational books such as fact books, scientific guides, atlases, and cookbooks?

- Do we have a special place for storing books and sharing them together? Do I encourage my child to engage in the books and print in our home?

- Do we have a library card and make frequent trips to the library? [*Note:* Many libraries allow families to check out as many as thirty books every two weeks; it's truly the best bargain in town!]

- Do I encourage my child to develop a love affair with books—and choose books that my child loves best while introducing new books and authors that I'm pretty sure my child will enjoy?

Promote Oral Language

- Do I talk with my child throughout the day about what I'm doing? About what my child is doing?

- Do I really listen to my child?

- Do I use interesting new words with my child and explain unfamiliar words?

- Do I tell my child stories about my day—and about our day together?

- Do I sing songs and share nursery rhymes with my child and invite my child to do the same?

Engage in Read-Alouds

- Do I read aloud to my child every day in ways that are comfortable and unrushed? Do I read with expression and model that reading aloud is fun? Do I encourage my child to ask questions and make comments as we read together? Do I use read-alouds to show my child how books "work"?

- Do I point out letters for my child to identify—especially the ones from my child's own name?

- Do I help my child understand that we can explore the world by reading, and by connecting the books we read to our own lives and to other books we've read?

- Do I reread my child's favorites—again and again as asked? Do I introduce my child to new books and authors?

- Do I use books as "learning partners" and as friends when my child is facing a challenge?

Promote Writing

- Do I provide my child with materials for writing and drawing such as a variety of papers, pencils, markers, and crayons?

- Do I encourage my child to write and draw?

- Do I encourage my child to write his or her name on the paper and praise whatever that looks like?

- Do I ask my child to read to me what he or she has written?

- Do I model writing in front of my child, discussing what I'm doing (for example, answering email, paying a bill, writing a letter)?

- Do I display my child's writing and other work?

Engage in Other Literacy Activities

- Do I have materials that enable my child to manipulate letters; for example, magnetic letters on the refrigerator, alphabet sponges in the tub, or rubber stamps and paper?

- Do I provide books on tape or book-based videos?

- Do I play games with my child that include possibilities for literacy development?

- Does my child have access to puppets and "dress-ups" and other ways to act out stories?

- Do I encourage my child to incorporate print in his or her pretend play? Do I take my child on walks or other outings and talk about the print we see? When I cook, do I invite my child to help read the recipe and prepare the food?

DON'T-MISS RESOURCES

Beyond Bedtime Stories:
A Parent's Guide to Promoting Reading, Writing, and Other Literacy Skills from Birth to 5

by V. Susan Bennett-Armistead,
Nell K. Duke, and Annie M. Moses

Taking a "literacy-throughout-the-day" approach, these three literacy experts organize the book around spaces in the home—the kitchen, bedroom, living room, and so forth—and suggest fun, stimulating ways to build your child's reading, writing, drawing, listening, and speaking skills in those spaces. Filled with tips, photos, milestones to watch for, and great ideas to try today, *Beyond Bedtime Stories* will not only help prepare your child for school, but also bring great joy into his or her life from birth.

It's Not Complicated! © 2012 by Phyllis C. Hunter, Scholastic

What else do I do to provide literacy opportunities for my child? What do I do to encourage my child's love of literacy and learning?

(Adapted from *Beyond Bedtime Stories*, 2004.)

WILLIAM AND CONNIE'S STORY

To get a firsthand look at the difference voluminous independent reading makes, meet single African American mom Connie, who reared her son, William, in the South without support from his father. Connie's motto is one we'd all do well to live by: *The family that reads together achieves together.* Connie began to read to William when he was just a few days old. She or other family members read him at least one story every day. Connie purchased books for him through a children's book club, and made biweekly trips to the library, checking out about a dozen books each time. When William was two, he began to participate in the summer reading program sponsored by the local public library, and by the time he started first grade, he had read himself—or others had read to him—more than 2,000 books. And that was just the beginning of William's remarkable reading life; he routinely read more than 100 books a year (typically each one more than 200 pages).

Approximately 47 percent of the students at William's public high school were eligible for free or reduced-price lunch. His 2007 graduating class was approximately 50 percent African American, 42 percent white, and 8 percent Latino and other ethnic groups. William's SAT Critical Reading Score was 780 and here's a comparison of his ACT reading score with other 2007 college-bound seniors:

William's ACT Reading Score Compared to Other 2007 College-Bound Students

William's ACT Reading Score	32
White ACT Mean Score	22.5
ACT Reading Mean Score for All Examinees	21.5
African American ACT Reading Mean	17.1

William currently attends college on scholarship. Connie is convinced that reading put her son on the level of a child who had attended exclusive private schools; for William, clearly reading was the great equalizer (Jairrels, pp. 96–104).

What the Research Says About Helping Our Kids Believe They Will Go to College

- Although the gap between African Americans and whites graduating from high school has narrowed over the last century, the gap between the percentage of African American and white people with college degrees in the U.S. population has been expanding almost every year since 1940.

- In 1940, only 1.42 percent of African American males had college degrees, compared to 5.8 percent of white males. In 2007, 15 percent of black males had a college degree, compared to 31 percent of white males.

- A CBS Poll found that most African American students want to go the college. Across races, about 65 percent of males and 75 percent of females planned to go to a four-year college after graduating from high school. More African American students regardless of gender planned to go to vocational or technical school, and more male students regardless of race planned to go into the armed forces.

- When responding to the question, "Would you say most of your friends probably will or probably will not go to college?" Black male and female students were significantly more likely to respond, "Will not." 40 percent of black males and 31 percent of black females stated that their friends probably would not go to college, compared to 23 percent of white males and females.

- When asked the question, "What do you think your friends would like more: if you go to college, or if you don't go to college, or your friends would not care either way?" African American students were more likely to report that their friends want them to go to college. White students were more likely to state that their friends wouldn't care either way.

- What factors discourage African American kids from pursuing college? More than one third of all African American students who decided not to attend college stated that they could not afford it. 10 percent of black males said that they did not have enough information about college.

- 15 percent of African American females elected not to go to college for "family reasons," compared to 0 percent of African American

It's Not Complicated! © 2012 by Phyllis C. Hunter, Scholastic

males. African American females were the most likely to report being stressed about college when compared to other race groups.

(CBS News/MTV/Gates Foundation Monthly Poll, March 2005 [Computer file]. ICPSR04322 v2. Inter-university Consortium for Political and Social Research; 2005.)

It's Not Complicated

As we work to pull all our kids up to grade level where they belong—full of the confidence they need to keep succeeding—we need to hold everyone accountable: schools, families, communities, and the government. Teachers can't go it alone. Dr. Patricia Edwards and Dr. Susan Piazza, writing in their *Education Nation* blog (11.8.11), remind us of researcher Gloria Ladson-Billings' wise words: Kids of color fail, in part, because of the "years of inequitable access to schools, health care, libraries, housing, and other sociological factors. Race, class, language, and other forms of difference create hierarchies of privilege and disadvantage that feed the achievement gaps."

But that need not be our legacy. As Alfred Tatum reminds us, *reading is our legacy*. Let's embrace reading as the glory it is . . . books invite us to explore worlds beyond what we can imagine, to see what's possible, and to understand that, in large part, we each shape our own destinies. Let us read to know that our destinies can be as productive and promising as we choose.

To this end, I never get tired of sharing the inspirational stories of young African Americans who read their way to success; here are three of my favorites:

The Pact

This is a uniquely inspiring story, one I never tire of revisiting. These three young men grew up on the streets of Newark, facing city life's temptations, pitfalls, even jail. But one day, they made a pact. They promised each other they would all become doctors, and stick it out together on the arduous journey through medical school to attain that dream. And to this day, Sampson Davis, George Jenkins, and Rameck Hunt are not only friends—they are also all doctors. Read it yourself for inspiration and find a way to share it with the kids in your life; they, too, can beat the odds.

Gifted Hands: The Ben Carson Story

Ben Carson, M.D., is one of the most celebrated neurosurgeons in the world. In *Gifted Hands*, he tells of his inspiring odyssey from his childhood in inner-city Detroit to his position as director of pediatric neurosurgery at Johns Hopkins Hospital at age 33. Ben Carson is a role model for anyone who attempts the seemingly impossible. Filled with fascinating case histories, this is a dramatic and intimate story of Ben Carson's struggle to beat the odds—and of the faith and genius that continue to shape his journey.

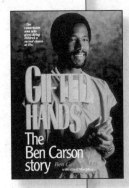

The Tom Joyner Foundation

The Tom Joyner Foundation (www.blackamericaweb.com/?q=tjf_tjfoundation) does only does one thing; it helps students continue their education at black colleges. All too often a student will get into college, then encounter financial difficulties that will force them to drop out. The Foundation provides money directly to the Historical Black Colleges and Universities (HBCUs) for the purpose of helping these students complete their education.

DON'T-MISS RESOURCES

African Americans and Standardized Tests:
The Real Reason for Low Test Scores

by Veda Jairrels, J.D., Ph.D.

What accounts for African American students' low scores on standardized tests? Dr. Jairrels believes she knows—in too many African American households, avid reading is not encouraged or supported. Typically, while most of the blame for a child's poor performance is placed upon the teachers, the curricula, and the social structure of the schools, Jairrels ultimately places the responsibility back in the hands of the family and offers suggestions for improvement.

Dr. Jairrels writes that in today's world, "Reading is the great equalizer." She suggests the number of books children should read under the tutelage of parents in addition to those assigned at school. Her recommendations are helpful for all who are eager to help children of color develop a reading habit including church goers, concerned citizens, and Black Greek sororities and fraternities.

"I'm going to inscribe on my tombstone: "She tried to put a book in the hands of every child!""

CONCLUSION

A Call to Action: Reading Is a Civil Right

*I*am an avid fan of the Saturday morning cooking shows on PBS. I have more than 1,000 cookbooks. One Saturday, after my cooking show wrapped, a show came on about tombstones and what people put on them. I decided right then and there that I would inscribe on mine: *She tried to put a book in the hands of every child!* This phrase, plus my birth date and *wife and mother* have already been carved on my tombstone because no matter how long I live these three things will never change.

When Our Children Can't Access Their Reading Rights

When six-year-old Mario can't read at the end of first grade because he doesn't understand the basics of decoding, is it his fault? No. When third grader Aisha fails and can't pass to fourth grade because she can't read, is it her fault? No. When seventh grader Arnold says he doesn't think he will go to college, is he lazy without ambition? No. These children are victims of a kind of child abuse—educational abuse, because they have not been able to access their reading rights:

- the right to access high-quality books
- the right to highly qualified teachers

- the right to a comprehensive reading program that teaches reading using the six essential elements: phonemic and phonological awareness, orthographic awareness, word study, comprehension strategies, and fluency
- the right to fair and credible assessments
- the right to college entrance information before sixth grade

Recognize good school leadership: it usually says, "Students come first, then content, and then the world."

What I Know for Sure About Avid Reading and Children of Color

I want to end this book on a high note. And that's easy to do because I've got my own knowledge about our students of color and reading—and the research to prove I'm right. Look what happens to our students when they read:

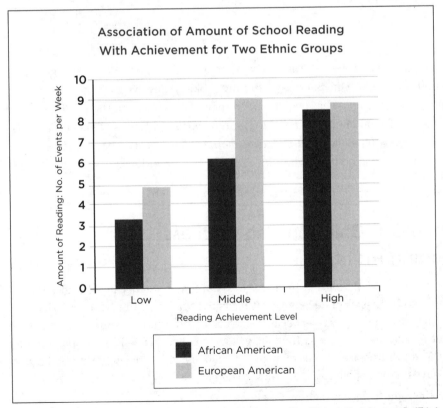

Association of Amount of School Reading With Achievement for Two Ethnic Groups

Swan, E., Coddington, C., & Guthrie, J. (2010). Engaged silent reading. Hiebert, E., & Reutzel, R. (Eds.). Revisiting Silent Reading. Newark, DE: International Reading Association, p. 101.

It's Not Complicated! © 2012 by Phyllis C. Hunter, Scholastic

When our kids read their hearts out, the so-called achievement gap all but disappears. Both white students and students of color perform off the charts when they've got hours and hours of avid reading backing them up.

Never forget: Good won't do when *great* is possible. Reading is our kids' civil right.

> *Whether or not people read, and indeed how much and how often they read, affects their lives in crucial ways. All of the data suggest how powerfully reading transforms the lives of individuals—whatever their social circumstances. Regular reading not only boosts the likelihood of an individual's academic and economic success . . . but it also seems to awaken a person's social and civic sense . . . Books change lives for the better.*

—Dana Gioia, Chairman,
National Endowment for the Arts, 2007

References

Afflerbach, P. (2008). Best practices in literacy assessment. In L. Gambrell, L. M. Morrow, & M. Pressley. (Eds.) (2007). *Best practices in literacy instruction*. New York: Guilford.

Allington, R. (2011). *What really matters for struggling readers, 3rd edition*. New York: Addison-Wesley.

Allington, R. (2011). What at-risk readers need. What students need to learn. *ASCD*. March 2011, Volume 68, Number 6, pp. 40–45.

Allington, R., McGill-Franzen, A., Camilli, G., Williams, L., Graff, J., Zeig, J., Zmach, C., & Nowak, R. (2010). Addressing summer reading setback among economically disadvantaged elementary students. *Reading Psychology*, (31) 5, 411–427

Allington, R. (2009). *What really matters in response to intervention*. New York: Addison-Wesley.

Allyn, P. (2011). *Pam Allyn's best books for boys*. New York: Scholastic.

Allyn, P. (2010). *The great eight: Management strategies for the reading and writing classroom*. New York: Scholastic.

Alonso, A. (2010). Fewer black males drop out in Baltimore schools. *EdWeek*. November 2. Retrieved from: http://www.edweek.org/ew/articles/2010/11/03/ 10baltimore.h30.html?tkn=LRBFdumDMMkV%2FdC3gFYy0 C3uGFsNZwyrb%2B36&cmp=clp-ecseclips

Alston, L. (2008). *Why we teach: Learning, laughter, love, and the power to transform lives*. New York: Scholastic.

Atwell, N. (2007). *The reading zone: How to help kids become skilled, passionate, habitual critical readers*. New York: Scholastic.

August, D., & Shanahan, T. (2006). *Developing literacy in second-language learners*. Mahwah, NJ: Erlbaum.

Baumann, J. F. (2009). Vocabulary and reading comprehension: The nexus of meaning. In S. E. Israel & G. G. Duffy (Eds.) *Handbook of research on reading comprehension* (223–246). New York: Routledge, Taylor & Francis Group.

Beck, I. L., McKeown, M. G., & Kucan, L. (2002). *Bringing words to life: Robust vocabulary instruction*. New York: Guilford Press.

Bennett-Armistead, S., Duke, N., & Moses, A. (2004). *Beyond bedtime stories: A parent's guide to promoting reading, writing, and other literacy skills from birth to 5*. New York: Scholastic.

Bentley, P. (2011). Black and minority children watch 50 percent more TV per day than whites (and almost 90 percent have sets in their bedrooms), study finds. *Daily Mail*. Retrieved from: http://www.dailymail.co.uk/ news/article-2001098/Black-minority-children-watch-50-cent-TV-day-whites-90-sets-bedrooms--study-finds. html#ixzz1RY317M9m

Biemiller, A. (2005). Size and sequence in vocabulary development: Implications for choosing words for primary grade vocabulary instruction. In A. Hiebert & M. Kamil, (Eds.). *Teaching and Learning Vocabulary: Bringing Research to Practice*. Mahwah, NJ: Erlbaum.

Blachowicz, C. L. Z., & Fisher, P. J. (2006). *Teaching vocabulary in all classrooms*. (3rd ed.). Upper Saddle River, NJ: Merrill/Prentice Hall.

Blanchett, W. (2006). Disproportionate representation of African American students in special education: Acknowledging the role of white privilege and racism. *Educational Researcher*, Vol. 35, No. 6, pp. 24–28.

Blevins, W. (2011). *Teaching phonics*. New York: Scholastic.

Block, C. C., & Pressley, M. (Eds.). (2002). *Comprehension instruction: Research-based best practices*. New York: Guilford Press.

Bosman, J. (2012). Children's book envoy defines his mission. *New York Times*. January 3. Retrieved from: http://www.nytimes.com/2012/01/03/books/walter-dean-myers-ambassador-for-young-peoples-literature.html?_r=1

Bradby, M. (1995). *More than anything else.* New York: Orchard Books.

Bromley, K. (1993). *Journaling: Engagements in reading, writing, and thinking.* New York: Scholastic.

Burrell, Tom. (2010). *Brainwashed: Challenging the myth of black inferiority.* New York: Smiley Books.

Calderón, M. (2005). Teaching English language learners: Instructional tools for mainstream teachers. New website for WETA/AFT joint project: www.colorincolorado.net

Canada, G. (1996). *Fist, stick, gun, knife: A personal history of violence in America.* Boston: Beacon Press.

Center on Media and Human Development. Northwestern University (2011). Children, media, and race: Exploring the implications of racial and ethnic differences in media use among children and youth. Retrieved from: http://cmhd.northwestern.edu/?page_id=9

Chall & Dale (1995). Word List. Retrieved from: http://www.readabilityformulas.com/new-dale-chall-readability-formula.php

Chamberlain, S. P. (2005). Recognizing and responding to cultural differences in the education of culturally and linguistically diverse learners. *Intervention in School and Clinic, 40*(4), 195–211.

Cho, K., & Choi, D. S. (2008). Are read-alouds and free reading "natural partners"? *Knowledge Quest* 36 (5): 69–73.

Cipielewski, J., & Stanovich, K. E. (1992). Predicting growth in reading ability from children's exposure to print. *Journal of Experimental Child Psychology, 54,* 74–89.

Clark, R. (2003). *The essential 55: An award-winning educator's rules for discovering the successful student in every child.* New York: Hyperion.

Coleman, D., & Pimentel, S. (2011). Publishers' criteria for the common core state standards in English language arts and literacy, Grades 3–12. CCSSO. Retrieved from: *Common core state standards for English language arts & literacy in history/social studies, science, and technical subjects* (2010). Washington, DC: Common Core Standards Initiative.

Cunningham, A., & Stanovich, K. (1998). What reading does for the mind. *American Educator*, 22 (1/2), 8–15.

Darling-Hammond, L. (2010). *The flat world and education: How America's commitment to equity will determine our future.* New York: Teachers College Press.

Duke, N., Caughlan, S., Juzwik, M., & Martin, N. (2011). *Genre: Reading and writing with purpose in K–8 classrooms.* Portsmouth, NH. Heinemann.

Duke, N., & Carlisle, J. (2011). The development of comprehension. In Kamil, M., Pearson, D., Moje Birr, E., & Afflerbach, P. (Eds.). *Handbook of Reading Research. Volume IV.* New York: Routledge.

Duke, N. (2006). Improving comprehension of informational text. Center for the Improvement of Early Reading Achievement. Retrieved from: http://www.google syndicatedsearch.com/u/ciera?q=Improving+comprehension+of+informational+text.+&sa=Google+Search&domains=ciera.org&sitesearch=ciera.org

Duke, N. (2003). Reading to learn from the very beginning: Information books in early childhood. National Association for the Education of Young Children. Retrieved from: http://journal.naeyc.org/btj/200303/informationBooks.pdf

Duke, N., & Bennett-Armistead, S. (2003). *Reading and writing informational text in the primary grades: Research-based practices.* New York: Scholastic.

Duke, N., & Pearson, P. D. (2002). Effective practices for developing reading comprehension. In A. E. Farstrup & S. J. Samuels (Eds.). *What research has to say about reading instruction.* (3rd ed.). Newark, DE: International Reading Association, pp. 205–242.

Duke, N., & Kays, J. (1998). Can I say 'Once upon a time'? Kindergarten children developing knowledge of information book language. *Early Childhood Research Quarterly, 13*(2). pp. 295–318.

Dweck, Carol S. (2006). *Mindset: The new psychology of success.* New York: Ballantine Books.

Dyson, A., & Sitherman, G. (2009). The right (write) start: African American language and the discourse of sounding right. *Teachers College Record* Volume 111, Number 4, 2009, p. 973–998 Retrieved from: http://www.tcrecord.org ID Number: 15228

Eckholm, E. (2006). Plight deepens for black men, studies warn: Growing disconnection from the mainstream. *New York Times.* Retrieved from www.nytimes.com/2006/03/20/national/20blackmen.html

Edwards, P., & Piazza, S. (2011). Behind NAEP reading scores, an education debt. NBC News. Retrieved from: http://m.educationnation.com/index.cfm?objectid=0D186F56-0A42-11E1-9CAC000C296BA163

Edwards, P. (2010). *Change is gonna come: Transforming literacy education for African American students*. New York: Teachers College Press.

Edwards, P. (1999). *A Path to follow: Learning to listen to parents.* Portsmouth, NH: Heinemann.

Ehri, L. C., Dreyer, L., Flugman, B., & Gross, A. (2007). Reading rescue: An effective tutoring intervention model of language minority students who are struggling readers in first grade. *American Educational Research Journal, 44* (2), pp. 414–448.

Elley, W. (2000). The potential of book floods for raising literacy levels. *International Review of Education,* 46 (3/4), 233–255. Doi: 10.1023/A: 1004086618679.

Feldman, K., & Kinsella, K. (2005). Narrowing the language gap. The case for explicit vocabulary. Scholastic Online for Educators, Professional Papers. New York: Scholastic.

Ferri, B. A., & Connor, D. (2005). In the shadow of Brown: Special education and overrepresentation of students of color. *Remedial and Special Education, 26*(2), 93–100.

Fertig, B. (2010). Raising classroom standards means ramping up non-fiction. Retrieved from: http://beta.wnyc.org/articles/wnyc-news/2010/oct/11/raising-classroom-standards-means-ramping-non-fiction/#

Fountas, I., & Pinnell, G. S. (2008). *When readers struggle: Teaching that works.* Portsmouth, NH: Heinemann.

Fountas, I., & Pinnell, G. S. (2006). *Teaching for comprehending and fluency: Thinking, talking, and writing about reading, K–8*. Portsmouth, NH: Heinemann.

Fowler, D. (2007, January 24). Report explores ways to bridge achievement gap. *The Examiner.* Retrieved from http://www.examiner.com/a523386~Report_explores_ways_to_bridge_ achievement_gap html?cid=rss-Baltimore

Freeman, Y., & Freeman, D. (2007). *English language learners: The essential guide.* New York: Scholastic.

Fryer, R. (2006). Acting white: The price paid by the best and brightest minority students. *Education Next.* Winter. Retrieved from: www.educationnext.org

Fryer, R., & Levitt, S. (2004). Understanding the black-white test score gap in the first two years of school. *The Review of Economics and Statistics* 86(2): 447–464.

Gallagher, K. (2009). *Readicide: How schools are killing reading and what you can do about it.* Portland, ME: Stenhouse.

Gambrell, L., Morrow, L. M., & Pressley, M. (Eds.) (2007). *Best practices in literacy instruction*. New York: Guilford.

Gioia, D. (2007). *To read or not to read: A question of national consequence.* National Endowment for the Arts. Washington, D.C.

Gladwell, M. (2008). *Outliers: The story of success.* New York: Little, Brown & Co.

Goldenberg, C. (2011). Reading instruction for English language learners. In Kamil, M., Pearson, D., Moje Birr, E., & Afflerbach, P. (Eds.). *Handbook of Reading Research. Volume IV*. New York: Routledge.

Greenhow, C., Robelia, B., & Hughes, J. (2009). Learning, teaching, and scholarship in a digital age. *Educational Researcher, 38*. 246–259.

Gruwell, Erin. (2007). *The Freedom Writers diary: How a teacher and 150 teens used writing to change themselves and the world around them.* (2nd ed.). Broadway: New York.

Guthrie, J. (2008). *Engaging adolescents in reading.* Thousand Oaks, CA.: Corwin Press.

Guthrie, J. (2004). Teaching for literacy engagement. *Journal of Literacy Research, 36* (1), pp. 1–28.

Guthrie, J., Schafter, W., & Huang, C. (2001). Benefits of opportunity to read and balanced instruction on the NAEP. *The Journal of Educational Research, 94*(3), 145–162.

Hart, B., & Risley, T. (2003). The early catastrophe: The 30 million word gap by age 3. *American Educator,* 22, 4–9.

Hart, B., & Risley, T. R. (1995). *Meaningful differences in the everyday experience of young American children.* Baltimore: Paul Brookes.

Hernandez, D. (2011) Double jeopardy: How third grade reading skills and poverty influence high school graduation rate. The Annie E. Casey Foundation.

Hiebert, E. (2011). Text complexity and how it applies in the classroom. Text Project. Santa Cruz: University of CA. Retrieved from: http://textproject.org/assets/library/powerpoints/Hiebert_2011-10-18_Text%20 Complexity-and-How-it-Applies-in-the-Classroom.pdf

Hiebert, E., & Reutzel, R. (Eds.) (2010). *Revisiting silent reading: New directions for teachers and researchers.* Newark, DE: International Reading Association.

Hill, S. (2009). Oral language and beginning reading: Exploring connections and disconnections. Urbana, IL.: Forum on Public Policy

Hofferth, S., & Curtin, S. C. (2003). Leisure time activities in middle childhood. Retrieved from http://www. childtrends.org/Files/Child_Trends-2003_03_12_PD_PDConfHoeffCur.pdf

Jacobs, T. (2010). Home libraries provide huge educational advantage. Miller-McClure. April. http://www.miller-mccune.com/culture-society/home-libraries-provide-huge-educational-advantage-14212/

Jago, C. (2011). Understanding the common core state standards. Scholastic Guest Speaker. March 28.

Jairrels, V. (2009). *African Americans and standardized tests: The real reason for low test scores.* Sauk Village, IL.: African American Images.

Johnson, B. (2010). *Sister to sister: Black women speak to young black women.* West Berlin, NJ: Townsend Press.

Keene, E., & Zimmerman, S. (2007). *Mosaic of thought, second edition: The power of comprehension strategy instruction.* Portsmouth, NH.: Heinemann.

Klingner, J. K., Artiles, A. J., Kozleski, E., Harry, B., Zion, S., Tate, W., Duran, G. Z., & Riley, D. (2005). Addressing the disproportionate representation of culturally and linguistically diverse students in special education through culturally responsive educational systems. Education Policy Analysis Archives, 13 (38) Retrieved from http://epaa.asu.edu/epaa/v13n38/

Krashen, S. (2012). Reading for pleasure. *Language Magazine.* Retrieved from: http://languagemagazine. com/?page_id=3031

Krashen, S. (2004). *The power of reading: Insights from the research.* Portsmouth, NH: Heinemann.

Laminack, L. (2004). *Saturdays and teacakes.* Atlanta, GA: Peachtree.

Lane, B. (2008). *But how do you teach writing? A simple guide for all teachers.* New York: Scholastic.

Layne, S. (2009). *Igniting a passion for reading: Successful strategies for building lifetime readers.* Portland, ME: Stenhouse.

Lee, Y., Krashen, S., & B. Gribbons, B. (1999). The effect of reading on the acquisition of English relative clauses. *ITL: Review of Applied Linguistics,* 113–114: 263–273.

Losen, D., & Skiba, R. (2010). Suspended education: Urban middle schools in crisis. Report from Southern Poverty Law Center.

Losen, D., & Orfield, G. (2002). *Racial inequity in special education*. Cambridge, MA: Harvard University Press.

McGill-Franzen, A., & Botzakis, S. (2009). Series books, graphic novels, comics, and magazines: Unauthorized texts, authorized literacy practices. In E. H. Hiebert (Ed). *Reading More, Reading Better* (pp. 101–117). New York: Guilford.

McKeown, M. G., Beck, I. L., Omanson, R. C., & Pople, M. T. (1985). Some effects of the nature and frequency of vocabulary instruction on the knowledge and use of words. *Reading Research Quarterly, 20*, 522–535.

McWhorter, J. (2001). *Losing the race: Self-sabotage in black America*. New York: Harper Perennial.

McWhorter, J. (2000) *Spreading the word: Language and dialect in America*. Portsmouth, NH: Heinemann.

Miller, D. (2009). *The book whisperer: Awakening the inner reader in every child*. San Francisco: Jossey-Bass.

Moll, L., Amanti, C., Neff, D., & Gonzalez, N. (2001). Funds of knowledge for teaching: Using a qualitative approach to connect homes and classrooms. *Theory Into Practice, XXXI, 2*, 132–141.

Moore, W. (2010). *The other Wes Moore: One name, two fates*. New York: Random House.

Murray, L. (2010). *Breaking night: A memoir of forgiveness, survival, and my journey from homeless to Harvard*. Los Angeles: Hyperion.

Myers, W. D. (1992). Quote from Scholastic interview with Walter Dean Myers, published in *Somewhere in the Darkness*. New York: Scholastic.

Nagy, W. E., & Herman, P. A. (1987). Breadth and depth of vocabulary knowledge: Implications for acquisition and instruction. In M. McKeown and M. Curtis (Eds.), *The Nature of Vocabulary Acquisition*, (pp. 19–35). Hillsdale, NJ: Erlbaum Associates.

Nagy, W., & Anderson, R. (1984). How many words are there in printed school English? *Reading Research Quarterly, 19*, 304–330.

Neuman, S. (2001). *Access for all: Closing the book gap for children in early education*. Newark, DE: International Reading Association.

Noguera, P. (2002). The trouble with black boys: The role and influence of environmental and cultural factors on the academic performance of African American males. In *Motion Magazine*. May 13.

O'Connor, R. E., Bell, K., Harty, K., Larkin, L. Sackor, S., & Zigmond, N. (2002). Teaching reading to poor readers in the intermediate grades: A comparison of text difficulty. *Journal of Educational Psychology, 94*(3): pp. 474–485.

Oher, M. (2011). *I beat the odds: From homelessness to the Blind Side and beyond*. Los Angeles, CA.: Gotham Press.

Polak, J., and Krashen, S (1988). Do we need to teach spelling? The relationship between spelling and voluntary reading among community college ESL students. *TESOL Quarterly*. 22: 141–146.

Pressley, M., & Afflerbach, P. (1995). *Verbal protocols of reading: The nature of constructively responsive reading*. Hillsdale, NJ: Erlbaum.

Rasinski, T., & Zutell, J. (2010). *Essential strategies for word study*. New York: Scholastic.

Ray, K. W. (1999). *Wondrous words*. Urbana, IL: National Council Teachers of English.

Reutzel, D., & Gikkubgsworth, P. (1991). Reading time in school: Effect on fourth graders' performance on a criterion-referenced comprehension test. *Journal of Educational Research, 84*: 170–176.

Rodriguez, G., & Cruz, L. (2009). The transition to college of English learner and undocumented immigrants: Resource and policy implications. Teachers College Record, v111 n10 (2385–2418).

Schott Foundation Report (2010). *Yes we can: The Schott Report on public education and black males*. Cambridge, MA: Schott Foundation.

Scott, J., Skobel, B., & Wells, J. (2008). *The word-conscious classroom: Building the vocabulary readers and writers need*. New York: Scholastic.

Sieff, K. (2011). Washington-area schools confront the 'gifted gap.' *Washington Post.* November 6. Retrieved from: http://www.washingtonpost.com/local/education/2011/11/06/gIQAeYImtM_story.html

Smith, M., & Wilhelm, J. (2002). *Reading don't fix no Chevys.* Portsmouth, NH: Heinemann.

Squires, J. R., (2004). Extensive reading. In Cawelti, G., (Ed.). *Handbook of Research on Improving Student Achievement.* (3rd ed.). Arlington, VA: Educational Research Service, p. 126.

Stahl, S. (2005). *Teaching word meanings.* Hillsdale, NJ: Lawrence Erlbaum Associates.

Stanovich, K. (2003). Cognitive science: The conceptual components of reading & what reading does for the mind. Retrieved from: http://www.childrenofthecode.org/interviews/stanovich.htm

Stillwell, R. (2010). *Public school graduates and dropouts from the common core of data: School year 2007–08* (NCES 2010-341). National Center for Education Statistics, Institute of Education Sciences, U.S. Department of Education. Washington, DC.

Swan, E., Coddington, C., & Guthrie, J. (2010). Engaged silent reading. Hiebert, E., & Reutzel, R. (Eds.). *Revisiting Silent Reading.* Newark, DE: International Reading Association, p. 101.

Tatum, A. W. (2012). *Fearless voices: Engaging a new generation of African American adolescent male writers.* New York: Scholastic.

Tatum, A. W. (2009). *Reading for their life: Rebuilding the textual lineages of African American adolescent males.* Portsmouth, NH: Heinemann.

Taylor, B. M., Pearson, P. D., Clark, K., & Walpole, S. (2000) Effective schools and accomplished teachers: Lessons about primary-grade reading instruction in low-income schools. *Elementary School Journal,* 101, 121–165.

Todd, R. J. (2001). Transitions for preferred futures of school libraries. Keynote paper, IASL Conference, Auckland, New Zealand, 9–12 July, 2001. Retrieved from www.iasl-slo.org/ virtualpaper2001.html

Tough, P. (2008). *Whatever it takes: Geoffrey Canada's quest to change Harlem and America.* New York: Houghton Mifflin.

Trelease, J. (2006). *The read-aloud handbook.* (6th ed.). New York: Penguin.

Vandergrift, J., & Greene, A. (September 1992). Rethinking parent involvement. *Educational Leadership,* 50(1), 57–59.

Walczyk, J. J., & Griffith-Ross, D. A. (2007). How important is reading skill fluency for comprehension? *Reading Teacher,* 60, 560–569.

Wenglinsky, H. (2003). Using large-scale research to gauge the impact of instructional practices on student reading comprehension: An exploratory study. *Education Policy Analysis Archives,* 11, p. 19.

Whitehurst, G. (1992). Dialogic reading: An effective way to read to preschoolers. Retrieved from: http://www.readingrockets.org/article/400/

Winfrey, O. (2008). Oprah still stunned by own fame, ABC, Retrieved from: http://abcnews.go.com/GMA/story?id=125013&page=2

Worthy, J., & Roser, N. (2010). Productive sustained reading in a bilingual class. In Hiebert, E. & Reutzel, R., (Eds.). *Revisiting silent reading: New directions for teachers and researchers*. Newark, DE: International Reading Association.

Yudowitch, S., Henry, L., Guthrie, J. (2007). Self-efficacy: Building confident readers. Engaging adolescents in reading. In Guthrie, John T. (Ed.). *Engaging adolescents in reading,* (pp. 65–86). Thousand Oaks, CA: Corwin Press.

Index

Note: Terms in italics, excluding titles, point to definitions within the text.